The Little Red Barn Baking Book

Small Bites with Big Flavor

Adriana Rabinovich

Clarkson Potter/Publishers

New York

This book is mostly dedicated to Marc, who is the love of my life. Any residual crumbs are dedicated to Oscar, the world's most noble and beautiful labrador.

Thank you to Louise Cantrill, whose creativity and superior design skills were the catalyst for this entire project. Thank you to Carl Baldwin and Kaye Lyall for their dedication, skill, and commitment. Thank you to Barbara for all those bridge menus and for inspiring my love of baking. Thank you to Dalia for all those wonderful contributions and to Scott for lighting the damn stove in Giorgi. Thank you to Jeanine and Sophie for making me part of the family. Thank you to the Modlins for agreeing to have their photographs used and all of the relatives for allowing me to share pictures from the family album. Thank you to Tim Winter our photographer for allowing us to go crazy. Thank you to the team at Ebury Press and at Clarkson Potter. Thank you to Brenda and Geoff for their help testing recipes. A huge thank you to Polly Simpson for holding the fort at The Little Red Barn and for allowing me so much time out of the office. Thank you to all the staff, past and present, and to our suppliers at The Little Red Barn for all their hard work. Thank you to Les and Maisie for looking after Oscar. Thank you to Liz Robinson for helping me get The Little Red Barn off the ground. And finally a big thank you to all The Little Red Barn's customers for their support. None of this would have been possible without them!

Published by Clarkson Potter/Publishers, New York, New York.
Member of the Crown Publishing Group.

Random House Inc. New York, Toronto, London, Sydney, Auckland

www.randomhouse.com

CLARKSON N. POTTER is a trademark and POTTER and colophon are registered trademarks of Random House, Inc.

Originally published in Great Britain by Ebury Press in 2000.

Library of Congress Cataloging-in-Publication Data

Rabinovich, Adriana.
    The Little Red Barn baking book / by Adriana Rabinovich.
        p. cm.
    ISBN 0-609-80630-0 (pbk.)
        1. Baking. I. Title.

  TX763 R23 2000
  641.8'15–dc21
                                                      00-021583

ISBN 0-609-80630-0

10 9 8 7 6 5 4 3 2 1

First American Edition

Printed and bound in Singapore

Contents

Introduction   4

Muffins and scones   12

Cakes and frostings   28

Quick breads   48

Pies and strudels   62

Brownies   84

Cookies   92

Canapés, hors d'œuvres, and light snacks   110

Index   142

Introduction

Introduction • For best results • Basic techniques • Key ingredients
Staple ingredients • Equipment • Organization

Introduction

My very first cooking experience was when I was 5 years old. My grandparents had come from Philadelphia to visit us in South America. They always arrived with bags filled with edible goodies like freshly made bagels, smoked salmon, chocolate caramels, pretzels, and Oreo cookies. Amazingly, even with their suitcases filled like this, they still managed to bring fantastic presents for me and my two sisters.

On this particular visit they arrived with an Easy-Bake Oven. I remember the excitement when we picked them up at the airport, and I saw them emerge from customs with a very large box. The fact that this was for me was thrilling. I didn't care that my sisters' presents weren't so immediately visible. I attempted to haul the big box to the car myself, not wanting anyone else to interfere with the box or its contents.

When we arrived home, I couldn't wait to get the box open. Tearing furiously at all the bits of cardboard and plastic, I finally got to the little oven. It was the most beautiful pale lemon color, trimmed with bits of silver. From the outside it looked like a real oven, with a little window through which you could observe the cooking progress. It was powered by a 100-watt light bulb. The oven came with a few powdered cake mixes, an assortment of very authentic little cake pans, and some recipe books to get you started.

From the moment it was unpacked, the oven was in constant use. When all of the cake mixes were used up, I had to resort to scraps. My mother was a good source. Bits of pastry dough, chunks of tropical fruit, spoonfuls of batter left at the bottom of the bowl, and end bits of cookie dough were all gratefully accepted and dutifully converted into edible treats.

I was praised for my inventions and for being so resourceful. Upon offering grownups one of my delicacies, I would study their reactions. They had to be careful to disguise any hesitation, as I could smell a rat a mile away. I was highly selective as to who would taste the goodies – my sisters weren't allowed anywhere near the oven and were rarely offered anything. Only interested grownups, capable of giving an opinion, were offered the opportunity to try something. And, of course, once they had tasted something, they were immediately interrogated. Was it too sweet? Was the texture of the pastry too hard? Did they like the combination of mango and cinnamon? Would they like to have another taste? Had they ever tasted anything like it before?

Sadly, the little oven and I parted company when we moved house a few years later. But the joy and pleasure it gave me inspired me to pursue my love of cooking. Looking back now, that's really where my life as a product developer began.

I moved to England from America as a newlywed. It was an exciting time, living in a new country. But I came to realize that although the English and Americans share the same language, there are many social and cultural differences between us. At first I found it hard to understand or even recognize these differences.

While I was waiting for my official papers, it wasn't possible for me to work, so I had plenty of time during the day to familiarize myself with my new surroundings. My main preoccupation was to find new and interesting things to eat. I would wander around Reading, where we were living, looking for good food stores. I first found a delicatessen, who introduced me to a fantastic butcher, who recommended a helpful greengrocer. I became well known to all of them, and a frequent patron.

My requests for Karo corn syrup, Baker's unsweetened chocolate and bagels always turned into lengthy conversations. I would tell them how I would use these typically American products, and they would in turn introduce me to typically English items like Double Gloucester and Red Leicester cheeses.

My pronunciation was met with an awkward silence. I knew something I said was wrong, but they were always too polite to correct me. It was only when I came home and would gleefully recount all my purchases that I was made aware of my ignorance. No, it's not Glaw-sester cheese, it's Glor-ster cheese; not Lie-sester cheese, but Le-ster cheese. So, the Eliza Doolittle of the Oxford Road, Reading was born. I would practice what I was going to say en route to the market: one pound of tom-ah-toes, one pound of sprouts (never say Brussels in front of the word sprout), one pound of courgettes (never ever say zucchini), and so on.

When I got my first job, my market expeditions became less frequent. I worked for a small design company, located just behind the Royal Albert Hall in London. I had a stunning view from my office window. Unfortunately, the job lasted only about six weeks. I was fired for making lousy tea.

I soon recovered and moved on to bigger and better things. I joined a prestigious corporate identity company. They had a fantastic staff diningroom in the basement, where delicious food was served and lovely Portuguese ladies made you tea and coffee. They also had the best croissants and pains au chocolat for breakfast I've ever tasted, made with pure butter. The pastry just shattered into buttery flakes everywhere when you took a bite. I munched my way through many delicious lunches and made friends with the many different chefs over the years.

Eventually I followed my true instincts, and enrolled at Leith's School of Food and Wine to do a full-time cooking course. Despite 30 years of cooking and baking, I must admit that I was not prepared for the day-to-day reality of what it takes to be a chef. It was a gruelling six months, and although I was a good student, I never achieved particularly high marks for any of my efforts. The main reason for this was that most of the time I would – consciously or unconsciously – leave out some of the ingredients in the recipes. At the end of each session, I would find a little pile of leftover ingredients under my workstation. As much as I tried to make myself stick to the recipes, I always had an urge to change them, just a little bit.

Having graduated from cooking school at the ripe old age of 35, my job prospects were limited. I began by doing some private catering work, and I managed to secure an eclectic bunch of clients. The menus would range from a very formal dinner party at Highclere Castle, to Freudian-themed canapés for a group of psychiatrists, to a corporate ballooning tea party, held in the middle of a field. The only constant on the menu were my chocolate brownies. And these were always commented on.

Marc, my husband, watched my progress over several months. Although he loved hearing all the tales of near disasters and drunken guests, he was growing tired of eating leftovers. That's when he hatched his plan. He came up with a business idea, and that's how The Little Red Barn was born.

The concept was very simple: real American brownies. At that time, commercial brownies in the UK were nothing at all like a brownie should be. They were spongy squares of mediocre chocolate cake, with synthetic chocolate frosting. I had always complained bitterly that these abominations were allowed even to be called brownies, and this was a recurring topic of conversation with my many American friends in England.

Having made brownies, to great critical acclaim, since the age of about seven, I was confident that my product was better than anything else on the market. I was less confident about my selling abilities, so I asked my friend Liz Robinson to help me. She got me the names of the food buyers at the ten places in London where I wanted to see my brownies on the shelf. A few weeks later, armed with ten small bags of samples, we drove around London. Liz would jump out to deliver the parcels while I kept the motor running. When we got home, there were six orders on the answering machine. We knew we had a winner.

Since those early days, not a lot has changed at The Little Red Barn. While the company has grown bigger, the inherent values and commitment to quality have remained constant. Every product continues to be developed in my kitchen and is put through the same rigorous taste-test process – very similar to the days of the Easy-Bake Oven. What's most important to me is that the integrity, spirit and quality of our products don't get compromised along the way.

So, when I was asked to write a cookbook, it was difficult to think what I could do that would be significantly different from what's already out there. Once again, husband Marc provided me with the solution: "The difference is you." So there it is. This is very much a cookbook about me. It contains lots of treasured memories about food, family and friends, along with lots of good recipes for everyday baking. These are simple recipes that have transformed and enriched my life, and I hope they'll do the same for you.

Happy baking!

For best results...

There are many people out there who will tell you that baking is a precise science. They'll tell you that sticking to the rules and slavishly following recipes are the keys to success. Personally, I think this is nonsense. For me, the key to successful baking is enjoying the sheer pleasure of it and the pleasure it gives to the people you love.

I encourage you to experiment. Be bold and be creative. There's a certain amount of tolerance built into these recipes. If you need to substitute an ingredient, by all means go ahead. If it works, great. If it doesn't, well at least you've tried.

I won't bore you with rules and regulations or preach about the importance of technique. These are simple recipes that are easy to make and require only basic skills and rudimentary equipment. When a technique is critical to the success of the recipe, I'll let you know. Where I can shed some extra light or give you the benefit of experience, I've highlighted these areas for you.

Basic techniques

I've listed a few simple baking techniques to help you get the best results from these recipes.

Creaming: Use an electric whisk or wooden spoon. Bring the butter to room temperature and then beat the softened butter with the sugar in a large bowl until pale and fluffy. If creaming by hand with a wooden spoon, beat vigorously. Add the eggs into the creamed mixture, little by little, beating well after each addition. You want to achieve a consistency rather like mayonnaise. To prevent curdling, add a little of the measured flour to the egg and sugar mixture.

Folding: Sift the flour over the creamed or whisked cake mixture, sifting high so that plenty of air is incorporated. Using a large metal spoon, gently fold in the flour, cutting and gently folding it into the mixture using an over-and-under movement.

Kneading: Turn the dough out onto a lightly floured board. Fold it towards you, then push it down and away from you with the heel of your hand. Give it a quarter turn and continue kneading until the dough feels elastic and smooth, just like a baby's bottom.

Rubbing: Cut the butter or margarine into small chunks, then add to the flour and salt. Mix briefly with a metal spatula to coat the pieces with flour. Using your fingertips, pick up a small amount of the mixture at a time and rub the fat into tiny pieces. Do this as lightly and quickly as possible until the mixture resembles fine bread crumbs.

Whisking: Beat the eggs and sugar in a large bowl until the mixture is pale in color and thick enough to leave a ribbon-like trail when the whisk is lifted from the bowl.

Key ingredients

Good baking doesn't require lavish, expensive ingredients. But, like all things in life, it's worth getting the basics right. Choose your ingredients carefully.

Butter: All the recipes in this book were tested with unsalted (sweet) butter. It's worth being picky about the butter you use, as this has the most dramatic effect on the flavor and texture of baked goods. I buy the most expensive unsalted butter, because you can really taste the difference.

Flour: Flour varies greatly and can have a big effect on your results. Use a good premium-brand flour and buy it from a store where you know it hasn't been sitting on the shelf for months gathering dust. For most recipes, I use plain all-purpose flour. For recipes with yeast, use white bread flour, or strong flour.

Salt: I use sea salt or kosher salt for all my cooking and baking, as it has the best flavor.

Eggs: Don't economize on eggs. Buy farm-fresh, organic, or free-range eggs from a local supplier. All the recipes in this book use large eggs unless specified otherwise.

Staple ingredients

All the recipes in this book have been created using standard items available in a grocery store or supermarket. Although these are everyday staples, I strongly advise you to select them with care and attention. It will make your baking that much more delicious.

Flour and grains:
all-purpose flour
white bread flour
cornmeal

Dairy products:
unsalted butter
milk
eggs
buttermilk
cream (light or half and half, whipping cream)
crème fraîche or sour cream
cheese (Cheddar, Gruyère, Parmesan)

Sugar:
white sugar (superfine, granulated)
brown sugar (light and dark)
raw sugar (Demerara)

Leavening agents:
baking powder
baking soda
active dry yeast

Other useful items:
pure vanilla extract
vanilla beans
chocolate (semisweet, milk, white)
unsweetened cocoa powder
spices (cinnamon, nutmeg, allspice, ginger)
nuts (almonds, pecans, hazelnuts, walnuts)
dried fruits (raisins, apricots, cherries, cranberries, dates, crystallized ginger)

Pastry:
puff pastry: preferably all butter
filo pastry: preferably authentic Greek

Equipment

Ovens: Every oven has its own distinct personality which you really get to discover when you're into baking. Take time to get to know your oven and understand its moods and quirks. If you're unsure of its true intentions, invest in an oven thermometer to monitor the temperature.

Electric mixers: Despite having a cupboard full of gadgets and machines, I tend to use very few of these when I bake. An electric mixer is very handy for creaming butter and sugar, and for whisking egg whites into meringue. Other than that, I stick to the old-fashioned method of a wooden spoon and a mixing bowl. I enjoy the physical aspect of this as well as the nostalgia it evokes. It doesn't take that much longer to do it by hand and it saves time on the washing-up.

Baking pans: It's worth investing in a good selection of pans. Pick heavy-weight pans that won't buckle in high heat and that are easy to clean. If you invest well, they'll last a lifetime.

A standard assortment should include:

muffin pans
a 9-inch or 11-inch square cake pan
a selection of loaf pans
a selection of round cake pans
a large cake pan for celebration cakes

baking sheets
a deep-dish pie plate
a shallow fluted pie
pan with removable base
a springform cake pan

Utensils and other equipment:

a set of measuring cups
a set of measuring spoons
a set of mixing bowls (small, medium, and large)
a wire rack
parchment paper
plastic wrap
ceramic baking beans
cookie cutters
small canapé cutters

a balloon whisk
a rolling pin
a metal spatula
pastry brushes
a fine-mesh metal sieve
a flexible rubber spatula
sturdy wooden spoons
a large metal spoon

Organization

It's important to keep your wits about you when you're baking, as an omission can have dire consequences. I recommend that you read the recipe through first, before you start, and then assemble and measure out all the ingredients. This is the most time-consuming bit. Once you have everything to hand, you can get on with the recipe very quickly. Certain recipes require speed. This is because once the liquid is in contact with the leavening agents (baking powder or baking soda) it activates the rising process. The longer you take to get the mixture in the oven, the more of the leavening ability you're likely to lose. So don't hang around at this stage.

Blueberry muffins with streusel topping • Beth's banana maple muffins • Buttermilk cherry muffins • Corn muffins

Muffins and scones

Swampscott baking powder biscuits • Jumbo cherry scones
Cheddar cheese scones • Cinnamon buns • Popovers

As a student in Bennington, Vermont, my friends and I would frequent the local diner for the "early bird" hunter's breakfast, served from 3.30-5am. The homemade corn muffins there were legendary, and we used to brave the freezing temperatures just to have muffins and coffee – with endless refills, of course.

Some 15 years later, our weekend guests are treated to a similar experience. Still sleepy, they're drawn from their beds in the morning by the wonderful smells emerging from the kitchen.

A freshly baked muffin should have a craggy domed top and the outer texture should be crisp. As you pull the muffin apart with your hands, you should release a little puff of steam that carries the aroma of the fruit. Inside the texture should be light and moist. Be generous with the fruit and leave the pieces large to ensure that every bite contains a juicy sweet chunk surrounded by buttery muffin.

Once baked, let the muffins rest out of the oven for a few minutes before placing them in a cloth-lined basket. Serve them with butter, maple syrup, or preserves, and, of course, lots and lots of freshly brewed hot coffee. Any leftovers can be sliced in half and toasted face down in a hot frying pan or on a griddle.

☀ Tips for making great muffins:

Muffins are simple to make, but you need to observe three basic rules:

1 Don't overmix the batter.

2 Work quickly once you add the dry ingredients to the egg and butter mixture.

3 Be precise with the baking time, as a few extra minutes in the oven can mean dry muffins.

Blueberry muffins with streusel topping

A slightly crunchy, oatmeal topping sets off these classic blueberry muffins. Look for fresh, succulent blueberries which are bursting with flavor. If you're a real blueberry lover, try lightly crushing half the blueberries before adding them to the batter. This will intensify the blueberry taste.

For the muffins

⅔ cup milk
1 tablespoon white wine or cider vinegar
2½ cups all-purpose flour
2¼ teaspoons baking powder
¼ teaspoon grated nutmeg
¼ teaspoon ground cinnamon
½ teaspoon salt
⅔ cup (1¼ sticks) unsalted butter
⅔ cup granulated sugar
3 eggs, lightly beaten
1 cup fresh blueberries

For the streusel topping

⅓ cup light brown sugar, tightly packed
2 tablespoons all-purpose flour
3 tablespoons unsalted butter
½ cup rolled oats

Method

Preheat the oven to 350°F. Combine the milk and vinegar in a small bowl, and allow to stand for 10 minutes. Meanwhile, lightly grease a 6-cup (large size) or 12-cup (standard size) muffin pan.

To make the streusel topping, combine the sugar and flour. Cut in the butter, using a knife, until the mixture just starts to hold together. Add the oats. Set aside.

To make the muffins, sift the flour, baking powder, spices, and salt into a large bowl. In a separate bowl, using an electric mixer, cream the butter with the sugar until pale and fluffy. Add the eggs, little by little, and beat until smooth. The mixture should have the consistency of mayonnaise. Gradually fold in the sifted dry ingredients alternately with the milk mixture. Mix until just combined. Gently fold in the blueberries.

Working quickly, divide the batter evenly among the prepared muffin cups and sprinkle the tops with the streusel mixture. Bake for 25–30 minutes for large muffins, or 15–20 minutes for standard-size muffins, or until well risen and golden. Test if they are cooked through by inserting a wooden skewer: when withdrawn there should be just a few moist crumbs on it. Allow the muffins to cool in the pans for a few minutes before serving.

Makes 6–8 large or 12–16 standard-size muffins

Beth's banana maple muffins

My friend Beth's love of bananas was the inspiration for this recipe. She was expecting her first baby when she and husband, Nigel, came to spend the weekend. The next morning I surprised her with some freshly baked banana muffins. She loved them, and she always says she is very proud to have a muffin named after her.

Ingredients

⅔ cup milk

1 tablespoon white wine or cider vinegar

2½ cups all-purpose flour

2¼ teaspoons baking powder

½ teaspoon salt

3 eggs

2 teaspoons maple syrup

⅔ cup (1¼ sticks) unsalted butter

⅔ cup granulated sugar

1 medium–large ripe banana, cut into chunks

Raw sugar, for sprinkling

Method

Preheat the oven to 350°F. Combine the milk and vinegar in a small bowl, and allow to stand for 10 minutes. Meanwhile, lightly grease a 6-cup (large size) or 12-cup (standard size) muffin pan.

Sift the flour, baking powder, and salt into a large bowl. In a separate bowl, lightly beat the eggs with the maple syrup. In another bowl, using an electric mixer, cream the butter with the sugar until pale and fluffy. Add the egg mixture, little by little, and beat until smooth. The mixture should have the consistency of mayonnaise. Gradually fold in the sifted dry ingredients alternately with the milk mixture. Mix until just combined. Gently fold in the banana chunks.

Working quickly, divide the batter evenly among the prepared muffin cups and sprinkle the tops with the raw sugar. Bake for 25–30 minutes for large muffins, or 15–20 minutes for standard-size muffins, or until well risen and golden. Test if they are cooked through by inserting a wooden skewer: when withdrawn there should be just a few moist crumbs on it. Allow the muffins to cool in the pans for a few minutes before serving.

Makes 6–8 large or 12–16 standard-size muffins

Buttermilk cherry muffins

Okay, I admit, I have a thing about dried cherries. I am always looking for ways to sneak them into a recipe. They work particularly well in these muffins. It's as good a combination as strawberries and cream. The tangy, buttery base is just lovely with sweet, slightly tart cherries.

Ingredients

½ cup dried sour cherries

2½ cups all-purpose flour

2¼ teaspoons baking powder

½ teaspoon salt

3 eggs

1 teaspoon vanilla extract

⅔ cup (1¼ sticks) unsalted butter

⅔ cup granulated sugar

⅔ cup buttermilk or plain yogurt

Raw sugar, for sprinkling

Method

Preheat the oven to 350°F. Meanwhile, lightly grease a 6-cup (large size) or 12-cup (standard size) muffin pan.

Soak the dried cherries in ⅓ cup hot water for about 15 minutes.

Sift the flour, baking powder, and salt into a large bowl. In a separate bowl, lightly beat the eggs with the vanilla. In another bowl, using an electric mixer, cream the butter with the sugar until pale and fluffy. Add the egg, little by little, and beat until smooth. The mixture should have the consistency of mayonnaise. Gradually fold in the sifted dry ingredients alternately with the buttermilk. Mix until just combined. Drain the cherries, discarding the liquid, and gently fold into the batter.

Working quickly, divide the batter evenly among the prepared muffin cups and sprinkle the tops with the raw sugar. Bake for 25–30 minutes for large muffins, or 15–20 minutes for standard-size muffins, or until well risen and golden. Test if they are cooked through by inserting a wooden skewer: when withdrawn there should be just a few moist crumbs on it. Allow the muffins to cool in the pans for a few minutes before serving.

Makes 6–8 large or 12–16 standard-size muffins

Corn muffins

These delicious muffins are inspired by the legendary muffins served at The Bennington Diner, in Bennington, Vermont. Serve them piping hot out of the oven or griddled for the full diner effect. Lots of fresh butter and redcurrant jelly make a great accompaniment.

Ingredients

⅔ cup milk

2 tablespoons white wine or cider vinegar

1¼ cups all-purpose flour

1¼ cups cornmeal

2¼ teaspoons baking powder

1 teaspoon salt

⅔ cup (1¼ sticks) unsalted butter

½ cup granulated sugar

3 eggs, lightly beaten

Method

Preheat the oven to 350°F. Combine the milk and vinegar in a small bowl, and allow to stand for 10 minutes. Meanwhile, lightly grease a 6-cup (large size) or 12-cup (standard size) muffin pan.

Sift the flour, cornmeal, baking powder, and salt into a large bowl. In a separate bowl, using an electric mixer, cream the butter with the sugar until pale and fluffy. Add the eggs, little by little, and beat until smooth. The mixture should have the consistency of mayonnaise. Gradually fold in the sifted dry ingredients alternately with the milk mixture. Mix until just combined.

Working quickly, divide the batter evenly among the prepared muffin cups. Bake for 20–25 minutes for large muffins, or 12–15 minutes for standard-size muffins, or until well risen and golden. Test if they are cooked through by inserting a wooden skewer: when withdrawn there should be just a few moist crumbs on it. Allow the muffins to cool in the pans for a few minutes before serving.

Makes 6–8 large or 12–16 standard-size muffins

Swampscott baking powder biscuits

These baking powder biscuits, similar to English scones, became part of my recipe portfolio after a Thanksgiving weekend spent with the family in Swampscott, Massachusetts. Following a sumptuous Thanksgiving meal, I was surprised to greet a hungry crowd at breakfast the next morning. With the help of my brother-in-law Scott, I rose to the challenge. I made the biscuits, he made the turkey hash. The combination was dynamite, and the biscuits were an instant hit.

These biscuits are great for breakfast, served with plenty of butter and honey. You can also serve them at teatime with preserves or with supper to accompany a bowl of hot chile con carne. Gentle handling is the secret to making them. The crisp top provides a sharp contrast to the creamy white, almost silky interior. The biscuits should literally melt in your mouth. And, for the full "wow!" factor, serve them piping hot, straight out of the oven.

As an ex-caterer, I'm always prepared for a cooking emergency. I keep a few basic recipes tucked inside my address book, and this is one of them. Made with staple cupboard ingredients – flour, butter and cream – they don't need fancy equipment and you really can make them anywhere.

Ingredients

2 cups all-purpose flour
1½ tablespoons granulated sugar
1 tablespoon baking powder

1 teaspoon salt
½ cup (1 stick) unsalted butter, cut into small chunks
¾ cup light cream

Method

Preheat the oven to 425°F.

Sift the flour, sugar, baking powder, and salt into a large bowl. Gently rub in the butter, using your fingertips, until well incorporated. Add the cream and gently bring the dough together with a metal spatula or fork. Work the dough gently into a ball and knead briefly on a floured board.

Roll out the dough into a flat disk about ¼ inch thick. Cut out 2½–3-inch rounds with a floured cookie cutter and place on an ungreased baking sheet. Bake for 10–12 minutes, or until golden. Serve immediately.

Makes 8–10 biscuits

Jumbo cherry scones

As an American, I'll never feel qualified to be an expert on the subject of making scones. However, having sampled them all over England, I can tell you with great authority that the best scones you will ever have are those you make fresh at home. Nothing bought commercially will ever compare to the absolute bliss of fresh scones straight out of your oven. Here's my culturally fused version, which features American dried sour cherries, buttermilk, and a hint of nutmeg. Make them giant-sized for big appetites.

Ingredients

½ cup dried sour cherries
½ cup buttermilk
1 extra large egg
3 tablespoons light brown sugar, tightly packed
1 teaspoon vanilla extract
2⅓ cups all-purpose flour

1 tablespoon baking powder
½ teaspoon baking soda
¼ teaspoon grated nutmeg
½ teaspoon salt
½ cup (1 stick) unsalted butter, cut into chunks
Milk, for brushing
Raw sugar, for sprinkling

Method

Preheat the oven to 400°F. Soak the dried cherries in ⅓ cup hot water for about 15 minutes. Meanwhile combine the buttermilk, egg, brown sugar, and vanilla in a small bowl. Set aside.

Sift the flour, baking powder, baking soda, nutmeg, and salt into a large bowl. Gently rub in the butter, using your fingertips, until the mixture resembles coarse meal. Drain the cherries and discard the liquid. Stir the buttermilk-egg mixture and cherries into the flour and butter mixture. Quickly gather into a dough. Knead gently on a lightly floured board until the dough comes together. If the dough seems very sticky, add a bit more flour until it's easier to handle. Don't overknead.

Pat out the dough into a flat disk about ¾ inch thick. Cut the disk into 8 wedges using a sharp knife. Brush the tops with a little milk and sprinkle with the raw sugar. Transfer to an ungreased baking sheet. Bake for 15–20 minutes, or until golden.

Makes 8–10 scones

Note: This recipe will also make 18 dainty teatime scones. Divide the dough into three equal portions. Pat out each portion into a disk, and cut each disk into 6 wedges. Brush the tops with milk and sprinkle with the raw sugar. Bake for 8–10 minutes, or until golden.

Cheddar cheese scones

For the savory-toothed people in your life, this is a great alternative to traditional scones. Serve this cheesy version split and buttered, or as a base for something more substantial. I like to serve them topped with prosciutto, tomato, and fresh basil.

Ingredients

2 cups all-purpose flour
1 tablespoon baking powder
½ teaspoon salt
1 teaspoon mustard powder

¼ teaspoon cayenne
1½ cups grated Cheddar cheese
1¾ cups whipping cream

Method

Preheat the oven to 425°F.

Sift the flour, baking powder, salt, mustard, and cayenne into a large bowl. Add the cheese and mix through. Add the cream and gently bring the dough together with a metal spatula or fork. Knead gently on a lightly floured board.

Pat out the dough into a flat disk about ½ inch thick. Cut out rounds using a 3¼-inch cookie cutter. Transfer to an ungreased baking sheet. Gather up the scraps, re-roll, and cut out more rounds until all the dough is used up. Bake for 15–20 minutes, or until golden. Allow the scones to cool for a few minutes, then eat immediately.

Makes 10–12 scones

Cinnamon buns

Oh my, what a treat! These remind me of Philadelphia and Rindelaub's Bakery just off Rittenhouse Square. Make these for someone really special for Sunday breakfast.

For the dough

2½ teaspoons active dry yeast
3 tablespoons granulated sugar
½ cup milk
2 tablespoons unsalted butter
1 teaspoon salt
3½–4 cups all-purpose flour
1 egg, lightly beaten

For the filling

⅓ cup light brown sugar, tightly packed
2 teaspoons ground cinnamon
½ cup chopped pecan nuts, lightly toasted
2 tablespoons unsalted butter, melted and cooled

For the glaze

1½ cups confectioners' sugar
3 tablespoons unsalted butter, melted and cooled
3 tablespoons milk

Method

To make the dough, dissolve the yeast and 1 tablespoon of the sugar in ½ cup lukewarm water. Set aside for about 5 minutes until foamy. Meanwhile, warm the milk in a saucepan. Add the butter, remaining sugar, and salt, and stir until dissolved. Remove from the heat.

Sift 3 cups of the flour into a large bowl. Add the yeast, warm milk mixture, and the egg, and stir to make a dough. Knead for 10 minutes on a lightly floured board, incorporating more flour as necessary, until the dough is soft, silky and pliable. Form into a ball. Place in a buttered bowl and turn to coat the dough all over. Cover with plastic wrap and leave to rise until twice its original size. This will take about 2 hours. At this point, the dough can be left overnight in the fridge, ready to use the next morning. When well risen, punch down the dough, then leave to rest for 10 minutes. Meanwhile, butter a baking sheet. Prepare the filling by mixing the sugar, cinnamon, and nuts in a small bowl.

Roll out the dough into a rectangle measuring about 12 x 9 inches. Brush with the melted butter. Sprinkle the filling mixture over the dough, pressing it in slightly. Roll up the dough like a jelly roll, starting at one long side. Using a sharp knife, cut the roll across into 12 equal slices. Arrange the rolls, cut-side up, on the prepared baking sheet. Allow to rise, covered, for at least 40 minutes until doubled in size.

Preheat the oven to 400°F. Bake for 15–20 minutes, or until well risen and golden. While the buns are in the oven, prepare the glaze (and get the coffee started). Sift the confectioners' sugar into a bowl. Whisk in the melted butter and enough milk to make a thick but pourable mixture. When the buns are ready, remove from the oven. Pour the glaze over them and leave to set for a few minutes before devouring.

Makes 12 buns

Popovers

These are my favorite breakfast food. Really easy to make, they're very light and just the thing to start the day. Serve them right out of the oven with preserves and butter, and lots of good strong coffee.

Ingredients

1 cup all-purpose flour
½ teaspoon salt
1 cup milk

2 extra large eggs, lightly beaten
2 tablespoons unsalted butter
2 tablespoons corn meal

Method

Preheat the oven to 425°F.

Combine the flour and salt in a large bowl. Add the milk and eggs, and whisk gently. Don't worry about any lumps. Divide the butter into 6 or 12 equal pieces and drop one into each cup of a 6-cup (large size) or 12-cup (standard size) muffin pan. Use the butter to grease the cups generously. Dust with the corn meal, shaking out any excess.

Divide the batter evenly among the prepared muffin cups. For large-size popovers, bake for 20 minutes at 425°F, then reduce the oven temperature to 350°C and bake for a further 15–20 minutes. For standard-size popovers, bake for 10 minutes at 425°F and a further 10–15 minutes at 350°F. Serve immediately.

Makes 6 large or 12 standard-size popovers

 ## Tips for making great popovers:

1 Don't overmix the batter. Any lumps will disappear.

2 Don't overfill the pans. Two-thirds full is plenty, which will leave room for the popovers to expand.

3 Keep the oven door shut. No peeking for the first 10–20 minutes of baking.

Shrimpy's chocolate cake • Devil's food cake • Chocolate chip cake
Marble loaf cake • Velvet butter cupcakes • Vermont maple cake
Traditional honey cake • Carrot graffiti cake

Cakes
and frostings

Banana rock cakes • Aunt Ruthie's cheesecake • New Year's Day
fruit cake • Buttercream frosting • Chocolate cream frosting
Cream cheese frosting • Burnt butter frosting

For me, cakes are what baking is all about. The smell of a cake in the oven has got to be one of life's real pleasures. My preference is for simple, old-fashioned favorites, frosted with buttercream and with a few simple decorative touches. I hate showy, fancy cakes that are all fluff and no substance. I prefer to go for maximum flavor and to keep the look simple and unpretentious.

I'm not one for following recipes and rules too religiously, but when it comes to cakes, you do need to measure the ingredients carefully and be accurate about pan sizes and oven temperatures. I won't scare you with lots of trouble-shooting tips, but I'll give you the basics so that you'll know what pitfalls to avoid.

☀ Tips for making great cakes:

1　Be organized. Read through the recipe first and make sure you have all the ingredients on hand before you start.

2　Remember to preheat your oven.

3　Check the oven temperature. Too hot or too low will make the cake coarse or uneven in texture.

4　Try to use the right size of pan as specified in the recipe. If you need to use something else, you'll have to adjust the baking time accordingly.

5　Measure all ingredients carefully. There is no room for guessing with cakes.

6　Don't overmix the batter. If you have used an electric mixer for creaming, mix in the dry ingredients with a large metal spoon using a folding technique.

7　Don't overbeat the egg whites. This will make for a dry cake.

8　Don't overfill the pans. Two-thirds full is plenty, as the cake will need space to rise.

9　Don't crowd the oven. Place cakes well spaced out so there is plenty of room for the hot air to circulate.

10 Don't overbake. The cake is ready when it springs back if slightly pressed in the center, or a wooden skewer inserted into the center comes out clean.

Shrimpy's chocolate cake

Shrimpy was the perfect grandma. She was small (hence her nickname), gray-haired with a wry smile, and a fantastic storyteller. To top it all off, she was an expert cakemaker. We kids would spend hours at her house, waiting patiently for something wonderful to come out of the oven. While we were waiting, she would tell the most amazing stories about ballerinas and magic slippers, and tropical steamboats crossing the Panama canal with rivers of hungry crocodiles snapping below.

This was Shrimpy's hallmark cake. It's chocolatey and moist, and simplicity itself. I like to frost it with Chocolate cream frosting (see page 47) and decorate it with lots of chocolate sprinkles.

Ingredients

1 cup milk

1 tablespoon white wine or cider vinegar

2¼ cups all-purpose flour

1 teaspoon baking soda

1 teaspoon baking powder

½ cup (1 stick) unsalted butter

1½ cups granulated sugar

2 eggs

1 teaspoon vanilla extract

½ cup unsweetened cocoa powder

1 recipe Chocolate cream frosting (see page 47)

Method

Preheat the oven to 350°F. Combine the milk and the vinegar in a small bowl, and allow to stand for 10 minutes. Meanwhile, lightly butter and flour a 9-inch round, 1½-inch deep cake pan.

Sift the flour, baking soda, and baking powder into a bowl. In a separate bowl, cream the butter with the sugar until pale and fluffy. Add the eggs, one by one, beating after each addition. Add the vanilla. Sift the cocoa powder into another bowl, removing any lumps. Gradually add ⅓ cup hot water, stirring to make a smooth paste. Fold in the sifted dry ingredients alternately with the milk mixture to the creamed butter and sugar. Mix until just combined. Fold in the cocoa paste.

Working quickly, pour the batter into the prepared pan. Bake for 35–45 minutes, or until a wooden skewer inserted into the center comes out clean. Leave to cool in the pan for 5 minutes before turning out onto a wire rack. Allow to cool completely before covering with Chocolate cream frosting and serving.

Makes 1 large cake

Devil's food cake

Very devilish and certainly chocolatey, this cake is dark and very moist. The secret ingredient is a chocolate custard, which is incorporated into the cake batter. If you want to make someone who loves chocolate happy, bake them this cake. They'll love you for ever and ever.

For the cake

2¼ cups all-purpose flour
1 teaspoon baking soda
½ teaspoon salt
½ cup (1 stick) unsalted butter
1 cup granulated sugar
1 teaspoon vanilla extract
2 eggs
1 cup full-fat milk
2 recipes Chocolate buttercream frosting
(see page 46)

For the custard

1 egg
½ cup full-fat milk
⅔ cup granulated sugar
1 cup chopped semisweet chocolate

Method

To make the custard, lightly whisk the eggs in a large bowl. Add the milk and sugar, and whisk until smooth. Pour the mixture into a small saucepan and stir over a medium heat with a wooden spoon until it thickens. This can take up to 15 minutes, so be patient. The custard should be pale and watery, or just thick enough to barely coat the back of the spoon. Remove from the heat. Add the chocolate chunks and stir gently until melted. Continue stirring over the heat until the chocolate custard thickens slightly. It should have the consistency of thin cream. Remove from the heat and leave to cool.

Preheat the oven to 350°F. Butter and flour a 9-inch round, 1½-inch deep cake pan. Chill in the fridge.

Sift the flour, baking soda, and salt into a bowl. In a separate bowl, cream the butter with the sugar until pale and fluffy. Add the vanilla and eggs, one by one, beating after each addition. The mixture should have the consistency of mayonnaise. Add the sifted dry ingredients alternately with the milk. Mix gently until just combined. Fold in the chocolate custard.

Pour the batter into the prepared pan. Bake for 20–25 minutes, or until the cake springs back slightly when gently pressed in the center. Leave to cool in the pan for 10–15 minutes before turning out onto a wire rack. Allow to cool completely before covering with Chocolate buttercream frosting. Using a serrated knife, slice the cake into three layers. Place some frosting in between the middle two layers to make a sandwich. Cover the top and sides of the cake with the remaining frosting. Leave to set for 1 hour before serving.

Makes 1 large cake

Chocolate chip cake

My sisters and I used to love going to Hesh's Bakery in northeast Philadelphia, Pennsylvania. No family birthday or celebration would be complete without one of Hesh's Chocolate Chip Celebration Cakes – a dense golden cake, somewhat like a Madeira cake, with zillions of chocolate chips magically suspended throughout and covered in thick, brilliant white frosting.

Thirty years on, Hesh's is still there, in the same location, with its striped awning, unmistakable neon sign, and an orderly queue of customers waiting to buy cookies, Danish pastries and cakes. Whenever I'm in Philadelphia I make it a point to visit Hesh's for a cake and several boxes of cookies. As I thought it unlikely they would share their recipe for chocolate chip cake, I devised my own version, which just might be better than theirs. (Not!) I prefer to make this cake at least a day before it's required, as the texture and flavor improve.

Ingredients

3 cups all-purpose flour
¼ teaspoon baking soda
½ teaspoon salt
1 cup (2 sticks) unsalted butter
3 cups granulated sugar

6 eggs
1 teaspoon vanilla extract
1 cup crème fraîche or sour cream
1½ cups roughly chopped semisweet chocolate
1 recipe Chocolate cream frosting (see page 47)

Method

Preheat the oven to 325°F. Lightly butter and flour a large cake pan that will hold about 3 quarts. Chill in the fridge.

Sift the flour, baking soda, and salt into a large bowl. In a separate bowl, cream the butter with sugar until pale and fluffy. Add the eggs, one by one, beating well after each addition. The mixture should have the consistency of mayonnaise. Add the vanilla, and fold in the crème fraîche. Fold in the sifted dry ingredients and chocolate chunks. Don't overmix.

Pour the batter into the prepared pan. Bake for 1 hour 20 minutes, or until a wooden skewer inserted into the center comes out clean. Leave to cool in the pan for 30 minutes before turning out onto a wire rack. Allow to cool completely before covering with Chocolate cream frosting.

Makes 1 very large cake

Note: For a standard-size layer cake, halve the recipe and use three 9-inch round, 1½-inch deep cake pans.

Marble loaf cake

When you can't make up your mind whether you're in the mood for chocolate or vanilla, this recipe makes the choice simple. Very moist, and lovely to look at, marble cake is just the thing when you're in need of a little comfort.

Ingredients

2 cups all-purpose flour

1 tablespoon baking powder

½ teaspoon salt

½ cup chopped semisweet chocolate

⅔ cup (1¼ sticks) unsalted butter

1 cup granulated sugar

3 eggs, at room temperature, separated

1 teaspoon vanilla extract

½ cup milk

Method

Preheat the oven to 375°F. Butter and flour a 9 x 5-inch, 3-inch deep loaf pan.

Sift the flour, baking powder, and salt into a large bowl three times. (This helps to incorporate air which gives a lighter result.) Melt the chocolate in a double boiler or bowl set over a pan of hot water (or you can use a microwave). Stir until smooth. Set aside.

In a separate bowl, cream the butter with the sugar until pale and lemon-colored. Add the egg yolks, one by one, beating well after each addition. Add the vanilla. Add the milk alternately with the sifted dry ingredients. Mix gently until just combined. In another bowl, beat the egg whites until they just form soft peaks. Add one-third of the egg whites to the batter and fold through until well incorporated. Add the remaining egg whites and gently fold in, using the minimum amount of strokes, until just combined. Transfer half of the batter into another bowl. To one half, add the melted chocolate and fold through to incorporate evenly.

Drop alternate spoonfuls of the vanilla and chocolate batters into the prepared pan. Run a sharp knife through the batters in the pan and swirl a couple of times to blend slightly. Bake for 25–30 minutes, or until a wooden skewer inserted into the center comes out clean. Leave to cool in the pan, on a wire rack, before turning out. Allow to cool completely before serving.

Makes 1 large cake

Velvet butter cupcakes

These cupcakes are the essence of childhood. Just sinking your teeth into a light buttery cupcake, and licking the buttercream frosting off the outer paper case, will make you feel like you're five again. Make these for the kids and sneak a couple for the grownups, then watch everyone's eyes glaze over with pleasure.

Ingredients

2 cups all-purpose flour
1 tablespoon baking powder
½ teaspoon salt
⅔ cup (1¼ sticks)
unsalted butter

1 cup granulated sugar
3 eggs, at room temperature, separated
1 teaspoon vanilla extract
⅔ cup milk
1 recipe Buttercream frosting (see page 46)

Method

Preheat the oven to 350°F. Prepare two 12-cup (standard-size) muffin pans with paper liners.

Sift the flour, baking powder, and salt into a large bowl three times. (This helps to incorporate air, which gives a lighter result.) In a separate bowl, cream the butter with the sugar until pale and lemon-colored. Add the egg yolks, one by one, beating constantly. The mixture should have the consistency of mayonnaise. Add the vanilla. Add the milk alternately with the sifted dry ingredients. Gently fold in, using a large metal spoon, until just combined. Don't overmix. In another bowl, beat the egg whites until they just form soft peaks. Add one-third of the egg whites to the batter and fold through until well incorporated. Add the remaining egg whites and gently fold in, using the minimum amount of strokes, until just combined.

Divide the batter equally among the prepared muffin cups. Bake for 15–20 minutes, or until a wooden skewer inserted into the center comes out clean. Leave the cupcakes to cool in the pan before turning out onto a wire rack. Allow to cool completely before topping with Buttercream frosting.

Makes 20–24 cupcakes

★ **Note:** This recipe will also make a simple layer cake, which is great for birthdays or a weekend dessert. Pour the batter into two buttered and floured 9-inch round, 1¾-inch deep cake pans. Bake for 20–25 minutes, or until a wooden skewer inserted into the center comes out clean. For a spectacularly simple and delicious dessert, cut it into wedges, drizzle with some chocolate sauce, and top with a few fresh strawberries.

Vermont maple cake

At last, here's a cake that really does taste of maple syrup. A word of warning, though: you'll need a whole bottle, and you must use the real thing.

Ingredients

2¾ cups all-purpose flour
1 tablespoon baking powder
¼ teaspoon salt
½ teaspoon grated nutmeg
1 teaspoon ground cinnamon
½ cup (1 stick) unsalted butter

1 cup light brown sugar, tightly packed
1 cup maple syrup
3 eggs
1 teaspoon vanilla extract
1 cup milk
1 recipe Burnt butter frosting (see page 47) or confectioners' sugar

Method

Preheat the oven to 350°F. Butter and flour a 9-inch round, 1½-inch deep cake pan. Chill in the fridge.

Sift the flour, baking powder, salt, and spices into a large bowl. In a separate bowl, cream the butter with the brown sugar until pale and fluffy. Add the maple syrup and mix through. Add the eggs, one by one, beating after each addition. The mixture should have the consistency of thick mayonnaise. Add the vanilla. Add the sifted dry ingredients alternately with the milk. Gently fold in until just combined.

Pour the batter into the prepared pan. Bake for 35–40 minutes, or until the cake is golden and springs back slightly when gently pressed in the center. A wooden skewer inserted into the center should come out clean. Leave to cool in the pan for 10 minutes before turning out onto a wire rack. Allow to cool completely before covering with Burnt butter frosting or simply dusting with confectioners' sugar.

Makes 1 large cake

Traditional honey cake

This is another recipe from my grandmother, Shrimpy. It was always on the holiday table during Roshashana and for breaking the fast after Yom Kippur. This is a light, airy cake with an excellent honey flavor. To make it extra special I like to serve it with tea done Russian-style, which means in tall glasses with silver holders.

Ingredients

¼ cup broken walnuts
¼ cup raisins
1½ cups all-purpose flour
1¼ teaspoons baking powder
1 teaspoon baking soda
½ teaspoon ground cinnamon
½ teaspoon ground cloves

4 eggs, at room temperature, separated
½ cup granulated sugar
½ cup honey
½ cup sunflower oil
½ cup strong tea (such as English Breakfast)
1 recipe Burnt butter frosting (see page 47) or confectioners' sugar

Method

Preheat the oven to 325°F. Butter and flour a 10-inch round, 4-inch deep tube pan. Chill in the fridge.

Place the walnuts on a baking sheet and toast in the oven until fragrant. Leave to cool for a few minutes, then roughly chop and combine with the raisins. Add 1 tablespoon of the flour and toss lightly. Set aside. Sift the remaining flour, baking powder, baking soda, and spices into a large bowl. In a separate bowl, beat the egg yolks with the sugar, using an electric mixer, until the mixture holds a ribbon-like trail on the surface. Add the honey and oil in a steady stream, and beat constantly. The mixture should have the consistentcy of mayonnaise. Fold in the sifted dry ingredients alternately with the tea, mixing until smooth. In another bowl, beat the egg whites until they just form soft peaks. Fold one-third of the egg whites into the cake mixture, using a large metal spoon, combining thoroughly. Fold in the remaining egg whites together with the walnuts and raisins. Don't overmix.

Pour the batter into the prepared pan. Bake for 40–50 minutes, or until a wooden skewer inserted into the center comes out clean, and the cake springs back slightly when gently pressed in the center. Leave to cool in the pan for 10–15 minutes before turning out onto a wire rack. Allow to cool completely before covering with Burnt butter frosting or simply dusting with confectioners' sugar.

Makes 1 large cake

★ **Note**: This is a light cake, so the nuts and raisins will sink to the bottom. It will still taste delicious.

Carrot graffiti cake

Eva, our cook in Colombia, used to make the best carrot cake. This cake has a similar texture and is very close to her version. The graffiti bit comes from a birthday cake I made for Marc. Not being very good at conventional cake decorating, I frosted the cake and then asked each of the guests to come into the kitchen and write a greeting. The results were lively – not always polite – and very festive-looking.

You'll need to use an electric mixer for this recipe.

Ingredients

2 cups all-purpose flour
2 teaspoons baking powder
1½ teaspoons baking soda
1 teaspoon ground cinnamon
1 teaspoon salt
4 eggs

1¾ cups granulated sugar
1¼ cups sunflower oil
2 cups grated carrots (about 3 large carrots)
1 recipe Cream cheese frosting (see page 47)
Tubes of ready-made writing icing, for decorating

Method

Preheat the oven to 350°F. Butter and flour two 9-inch round, 1½-inch deep cake pans. Chill in the fridge.

Sift the flour, baking powder, baking soda, cinnamon, and salt into a large bowl. In a separate bowl, using an electric mixer, beat the eggs at high speed. Add the sugar and continue beating until pale and fluffy. Add the oil in a steady stream, beating until the mixture holds a ribbon-like trail on the surface. Fold in the carrots, using a metal spoon, and then the flour. Don't overmix.

Pour the mixture into the prepared pans. Bake for 30–40 minutes, or until a wooden skewer inserted into the center comes out clean. Leave to cool in the pans for 10–15 minutes before turning out onto a wire rack. Allow to cool completely before covering with Cream cheese frosting. Place some frosting in between the two cakes to make a sandwich. Cover the top and sides of the cake with the remaining frosting. Decorate using tubes of ready-made writing icing. Keep it clean!

Makes 1 large cake

★ Note: This recipe will also make one very large round cake. Pour the batter into a buttered and floured 11-inch round, 2-inch deep cake pan. Bake for 40–50 minutes, or until a wooden skewer inserted into the center comes out clean.

Banana rock cakes

This is our mad designer, Louise Cantrill's recipe and it's a bit special. The "rock" bit is not a reference to the end result. It's more to do with how they make you want to "rock and roll" with pleasure after you've eaten them. I've copied the recipe just as she's given it to me. She's so clever.

Ingredients

1¾ cups all-purpose flour
1½ teaspoons baking powder
⅓ cup unsalted butter,
cut into chunks
1 tablespoon light brown sugar

⅓ cup golden raisins
½ cup chopped semisweet chocolate
1 cup ripe bananas (about 2 medium bananas)
1 teaspoon lemon juice
1 egg

Method

Preheat the oven to 400°F. Lightly grease a baking sheet.

Sift the flour and baking powder into a bowl. Rub in the butter until the mixture resembles your complexion after a night out. Add the sugar, raisins, and chocolate.

In another bowl, mash the bananas, pretending they're all the people you hate. Add the lemon juice and the egg, and mix well. Combine the bananas with the flour mixture to make a sticky dough.

Spoon the dough equally into 10 lumps onto the baking sheet. Leave some space for spreading. Bake for 15 minutes, or until the cakes are golden brown.

While they're cooling on a wire rack, slip into your fluffy mules, put some Burt Bacharach on your stereo, and apply a good smearing of lip gloss to oil up your mouth for the pleasure to come.

Makes 10 very tasty cakes

Aunt Ruthie's cheesecake

This is a very special recipe belonging to my Aunt Ruthie. I was introduced to it one year when we were visiting her and my dear Uncle Sam in Tel Aviv. After Shabbat dinner, this delectable cheesecake appeared on the table. It was after the first portions had been dished out and devoured that the theory of "straightening" was unveiled. We watched as my cousins Sabrina, Aviv, and Zevy, and Uncle Sam, took turns "straightening" the edges of the cheesecake until… guess what? There was none left. I must admit, we did our best to help too. It's a great concept and it tends to work extremely well on this delicious cake.

For the dough

2½ cups self-rising flour

1 scant cup (scant 2 sticks) unsalted butter, cut into chunks

1 cup granulated sugar

1 egg, lightly beaten

1 tablespoon fresh lemon juice

1 teaspoon vanilla extract

For the filling

1 cup crème fraîche or sour cream

¾ cup lightly whipped cream cheese

1 egg

1 cup granulated sugar

1 tablespoon grated lemon zest (optional)

Fresh seasonal fruit such as fresh dates, nectarines and peaches, cut into chunks

Confectioners' sugar, for dusting

Method

To make the dough, place the flour, butter, and sugar in a food processor and blitz until the mixture resembles coarse bread crumbs. Add the beaten egg, lemon juice, and vanilla, and mix until a soft dough is formed. Cover with plastic wrap and chill for at least 2 hours. Roll out two-thirds of the dough and use to line the bottom and sides of a 9½-inch springform cake pan. The dough will be very soft, so handle it carefully. Set aside.

Preheat the oven to 350°F.

To make the filling, beat the crème fraîche and cream cheese together in a bowl. Add the egg, sugar, and lemon zest, and mix until smooth. Place a layer of fresh fruit on the bottom of the pastry shell. Pour in the cheese filling, stopping just below the top edge of the pastry shell.

Roll out the rest of the dough to a round, and place on top. Pinch the edges together to form a seal. Bake for 1½ hours, or until the filling is set. Test to see if it's cooked through by inserting a wooden skewer: when withdrawn there should be just a few moist crumbs on it. Leave in the oven for 10 minutes with the door ajar, then remove to cool, still in the pan, on a wire rack. Allow to cool completely before serving. This cheesecake is best made the day before. When ready to serve, top with more fresh fruit and dust with confectioners' sugar.

Makes 1 large cake

New Year's Day fruit cake

One New Year's Day we decided to venture out in the cold sunshine to do some vigorous walking with friends. It was a beautiful brisk day and we set off in convoy across the Oxfordshire Downs. A few hours later, we returned to our cars, practically frozen and feeling hungry. From the boot of our car, I produced some individually wrapped portions of my homemade fruit cake. We each took turns gulping down hot coffee from a thermos and clutching at our silver parcels. Everyone looked rosy and really happy. This cake has now become an annual tradition and part of our New Year's Day ritual. Even if the weather is not good for walking, we curl up on the sofa, in front of a roaring fire, with the papers and a slice of fruit cake. Mmmm!

Ingredients

1½ cups golden raisins
½ cup dark rum
(or Cognac, sherry, or brandy)
¼ cup chopped candied cherries
¼ cup chopped mixed candied peel
¼ cup crystallized ginger, chopped into small cubes
¾ cup semisweet chocolate chips
1¼ cups all-purpose flour
½ teaspoon ground cinnamon

¼ teaspoon ground cloves
¼ teaspoon ground ginger
½ cup (1 stick) unsalted butter
½ cup light brown sugar, tightly packed
3 eggs, lightly beaten
1 tablespoon molasses
1 teaspoon grated lemon zest
½ cup ground almonds

Method

Soak the raisins in half of the rum for at least 30 minutes, but preferably overnight.

Preheat the oven to 325°F. Butter and flour two 9 x 5-inch, 3-inch deep loaf pans.

Mix the cherries, mixed peel, ginger, and chocolate together in a large bowl. Sift the flour and spices into a separate bowl. In another bowl, cream the butter with the sugar until pale and fluffy. Add the eggs, little by little, beating after each addition. Add the molasses. Fold in the sifted dry ingredients. Add the lemon zest, raisins, and the rest of the rum. Stir in the almonds and the fruit and chocolate mixture.

Pour the batter into the prepared pans. Bake for 40–50 minutes, or until a wooden skewer inserted into the center comes out clean. Leave to cool, in the pans, on a wire rack. Allow to cool completely before serving.

Makes 2 cakes

Note: This cake is best made several weeks ahead. It will keep for 2–3 months if stored in tin foil, tightly wrapped in plastic wrap, and kept in a cool pantry.

Frostings

I'm very puritanical about frostings. I like a straightforward buttercream or chocolate frosting, which allows the cake to shine through. I'm not keen on overdecorated cakes with lots of pretend flowers and sugary bits on top. For me, the cake should look mouth-wateringly edible and delicious. The frostings here are easy to make and consist mainly of butter and confectioners' sugar. Getting the right consistency can be tricky, so here are some tips.

☀ Tips for making perfect frostings:

1 Always, always, always use fresh unsalted butter.

2 Make sure the butter is at room temperature before you start.

3 Use a wooden spoon, not an electric mixer, to cream the butter with the sugar.

Buttercream frosting

This is a great all-round frosting that you can use for cakes and cupcakes. Experiment with different flavorings such as maple syrup, lemon, rum, or anything else that takes your fancy.

¼ cup unsalted butter, at room temperature
2 cups confectioners' sugar, sifted
⅛ teaspoon salt

3 tablespoons cream
1 teaspoon vanilla extract (or other flavoring)

Using a wooden spoon, cream the butter with half of the confectioners' sugar and the salt. Add the remaining sugar alternately with the cream to make a smooth frosting. Add the vanilla extract or other flavoring. The frosting should be easy to spread.

Makes enough for the top and sides of a 9-inch cake or the tops of approximately 24 cupcakes

Other flavors

• To make Chocolate buttercream frosting: add ⅓ cup unsweetened cocoa powder with the confectioners' sugar and substitute 1 tablespoon of chocolate-flavor syrup for the vanilla.

• To make Maple buttercream frosting: substitute 1 tablespoon real maple syrup for the vanilla.

• To make Lemon buttercream frosting: use crème fraîche instead of cream and add 1 tablespoon finely grated lemon zest.

Chocolate cream frosting

5 ounces semisweet chocolate
⅛ teaspoon salt
½ cup crème fraîche

Melt the chocolate in a double boiler or in a bowl set over a pan of hot water. Remove from the heat. Add the salt and crème fraîche, and stir until smooth. Leave to cool before using.

Makes enough for the top and sides of a 9-inch cake or the tops of approximately 24 cupcakes

Cream cheese frosting

1 cup cream cheese   2–3 cups confectioners' sugar, sifted
1 cup (2 sticks) unsalted butter   2 teaspoons vanilla extract

Beat the cream cheese and butter together thoroughly using an electric mixer. Add the sugar in thirds, mixing well after each addition. Test for the desired level of sweetness. Add the vanilla. Chill for 1 hour before using.

Makes enough frosting for a nice thick layer on a large cake

Burnt butter frosting

½ cup (1 stick) unsalted butter 1 teaspoon vanilla extract
2 cups confectioners' sugar   4 tablespoons light cream
½ teaspoon salt

Melt the butter in a saucepan over a medium heat. Continue to cook the butter over a moderate heat until it's a dark shade of nutty brown. This can take up to 15 minutes. Watch carefully so as not to burn the butter (despite its name, it isn't really burnt). When it has reached the right shade of brown, remove from the heat and leave to cool for a few minutes. Sift the sugar and salt into a large bowl. Pour the butter through a fine-mesh sieve into the bowl. Add the vanilla and cream, and stir vigorously. If the frosting is too thick to spread, add a little more cream or milk to thin. Leave to cool for a few minutes before using.

Makes enough for the top and sides of a 9-inch cake or the tops of approximately 24 cupcakes

Apricot, pistachio, and cranberry bread • Classic banana bread
Lemon tea bread • Date bread • Apple, cranberry, and pecan loaf

Quick breads

Zucchini and poppy seed loaf • Pumpkin gingerbread • Corn bread
Savory pumpkin bread

I've always been fascinated by the English ritual of tea. When we were children, we would often interrupt our playing to have tea. We would take out the miniature tea cups and saucers, and sugar bowl with white sugar cubes and silver tongs from the special cupboard facing the stairs. Then we would go in search of something good to eat to have with our "pretend" tea.

Waiting in the pantry cupboard would be a moist and flavorful banana bread, or a slightly chewy date and nut loaf, or maybe some delicious pumpkin bread. These would make dainty little sandwiches, spread with butter or cream cheese. Nine times out of ten, the loaves were ear-marked for a charity bake sale or as a welcome gift for someone or other. But we could generally twist my mother's arm to relinquish a loaf in honor of our tea party. She was normally very obliging as the breads were easy to make and she could make another one very quickly.

That's why, of course, these are called quick breads. Made with either baking powder or soda, there's no kneading or rising before baking. It's really just a three-step process: measure out the dry ingredients, add the liquid ingredients, and bake.

Quick breads are very versatile, too. They may be sweet or savory, or something in between. Serve them with butter, cream cheese, goat's cheese, or just on their own.

Apricot, pistachio, and cranberry bread

I'm not one for low-fat baking, as in most instances the omission of butter or fat makes for something dull and tasteless. I'd rather go without than eat something that has no flavor at all. This bread is an exception. The vibrant colors and flavors of the fruit and nuts seem to distract the tastebuds. (It's even nicer with a little butter spread on top.)

Ingredients

½ cup roughly chopped dried apricots
½ cup dried cranberries
½ cup shelled pistachios
2¾ cups all-purpose flour
1 tablespoon baking powder

2 eggs
1 cup granulated sugar
½ teaspoon baking soda
1 tablespoon grated orange zest
Raw sugar, for sprinkling

Method

Preheat the oven to 350°F. Soak the apricots and cranberries in about 1 cup hot water for 5 minutes. Don't overdo it, as you want the fruit to be firm, not soggy. Meanwhile, butter and flour a 9 x 5-inch, 3-inch deep loaf pan.

Place the pistachios on a baking sheet and toast in the oven for 5–8 minutes, until fragrant. Sift the flour and baking powder into a large bowl. Drain the apricots and cranberries, reserving the water. If necessary, replenish the water to make 1 cup again. In a large bowl, whisk the eggs with the granulated sugar. Add the baking soda and the reserved fruit-soaking water. Add the apricots, cranberries, pistachios, and grated orange zest. Fold in the sifted dry ingredients.

Pour the batter into the prepared pan and sprinkle with raw sugar. Bake for 40 minutes, or until a wooden skewer inserted into the center comes out clean. Leave to cool in the pan for 5 minutes before turning out onto a wire rack. Allow to cool completely before serving.

Makes 1 large loaf

Classic banana bread

Few things can be nicer than a cup of tea and a slice of banana bread. It's comfort food at its finest. This recipe is slightly lighter than most banana breads. If you're ever stuck for a last-minute dessert, this is great served with vanilla ice cream and a drizzle of chocolate sauce.

Ingredients

⅓ cup milk

1 teaspoon white wine or cider vinegar

2 cups all-purpose flour

1 teaspoon baking soda

½ teaspoon salt

½ cup (1 stick) unsalted butter

1 cup granulated sugar

2 eggs

1 cup mashed ripe bananas (about 3 bananas)

Method

Preheat the oven to 350°F. Combine the milk and vinegar in a small bowl and allow to stand for 10 minutes. Meanwhile, butter and flour a 9 x 5-inch, 3-inch deep loaf pan.

Sift the flour, baking soda, and salt into a large bowl. In a separate bowl, cream the butter with the sugar until pale and fluffy. Add the eggs, one by one, beating well after each addition. Fold in the mashed bananas. Add the sifted dry ingredients alternately with the milk mixture. Mix until just combined.

Pour the mixture into the prepared pan. Bake for 50–60 minutes, or until a wooden skewer inserted into the center comes out clean. Leave to cool in the pan for 5 minutes before turning out onto a wire rack. Allow to cool completely before serving.

Makes 1 large loaf

★ **Note:** To build the chocolate directly into the recipe, add ⅓ cup semisweet chocolate chips to the batter, just before baking. If you're as addicted to chocolate as I am, you'll absolutely love it.

Lemon tea bread

This makes a really moist loaf that positively zings with lemon flavor. If you want a real treat, serve this with a cup of Marc's 45-minute espresso (see page 83), made on the flame of love!

For the bread

2 extra large eggs
Finely grated zest of 1 large lemon
3 tablespoon lemon juice
Pinch of salt
1 scant cup granulated sugar
⅓ cup crème fraîche (sour cream or plain yogurt)
1¼ cups all-purpose flour
2½ teaspoons baking powder
¼ cup unsalted butter, melted

For the lemon drizzle frosting

1 cup confectioners' sugar
Juice of 1 lemon
Pinch of salt

Method

Preheat the oven to 400°F. Butter and flour a 9 x 5-inch, 3-inch deep loaf pan.

To make the bread, whisk together the eggs, lemon zest and juice, salt, and granulated sugar in a large bowl. Fold in the crème fraîche, flour, and baking powder. Gently fold in the melted butter, mixing until just combined.

Pour the batter into the prepared pan. Bake for 8 minutes, then lower the oven temperature to 325°F and bake for a further 25–30 minutes, or until a wooden skewer inserted in the center comes out clean. Leave to cool in the pan for 5 minutes before turning out onto a wire rack.

To make the frosting, sift the confectioners' sugar into a large bowl. Add the lemon juice and salt, and stir until smooth. Adjust the sweetness by adding more lemon juice or more sugar as required. Drizzle the frosting over the warm bread and allow to set before serving.

Makes 1 large loaf

Date bread

Dense, chewy, and not too sweet, this bread makes terrific sandwiches, particularly spread with organic cream cheese. Use Medjool dates if possible, as they're a lot nicer than the standard kind.

Ingredients

3 cups all-purpose flour
½ cup granulated sugar
½ teaspoon salt
1 tablespoon baking powder
1¼ cups milk

1 egg, lightly beaten
6 tablespoons unsalted butter, melted
1 cup coarsely chopped dates
2 tablespoon grated lemon zest

Method

Preheat the oven to 375°F. Butter and flour a 9 x 5-inch, 3-inch deep loaf pan.

Sift the flour, sugar, salt, and baking powder into a large bowl. Make a well in the center. Add the milk and egg, and mix thoroughly. Add the melted butter together with the chopped dates and lemon zest, and stir to mix.

Pour the batter into the prepared pan. Bake for 45 minutes, or until a wooden skewer inserted into the center comes out clean. Leave to cool in the pan for 5 minutes before turning out onto a wire rack. Allow to cool completely before serving.

Makes 1 large loaf

Apple, cranberry, and pecan loaf

This quick bread has an unusual texture. It's best eaten the day after it's made, so that the flavors have time to develop, and you get lovely hints of apple, lemon, and buttery pecans in each mouthful.

Ingredients

½ cup pecans

2 tablespoons milk

¼ teaspoon white wine or cider vinegar

1¼ cups coarsley chopped Granny Smith apple (with skin)

Lemon juice

2 cups all-purpose flour

½ teaspoon baking soda

1 teaspoon baking powder

½ teaspoon salt

½ cup (1 stick) unsalted butter

1¼ cups granulated sugar

2 eggs

1 cup dried cranberries

1 tablespoon grated lemon zest

Method

Preheat the oven to 325°F. Butter and flour a 9 x 5-inch, 3-inch deep loaf pan.

Place the pecans on a baking sheet and toast in the oven for 7–10 minutes until fragrant. Leave to cool for a few minutes, then roughly chop. Combine the milk and vinegar and allow to stand for 5 minutes. Meanwhile, place the apples in a large bowl and sprinkle with a little lemon juice to stop them discoloring.

Sift the flour, baking soda, baking powder, and salt into a large bowl. In a separate bowl, cream the butter with the sugar until pale and lemon-colored. Add the eggs, one by one, beating well after each addition. The mixture should have the consistency of mayonnaise. Add the sifted dry ingredients alternately with the milk mixture. Fold in the chopped apple, chopped pecans, dried cranberries, and lemon zest. Don't overmix.

Working quickly, pour the batter into the prepared pan. Bake for 45–50 minutes, or until a wooden skewer inserted into the center comes out clean. Leave to cool in the pan for 5 minutes before turning out onto a wire rack. Allow to cool completely before serving.

Makes 1 large loaf

Zucchini and poppy seed loaf

You say zucchini, I say courgette! This loaf works on a similar principle to carrot cake, with zucchini adding moistness, flecks of color and a nice hint of spice. The bread is perfect with a cup of tea.

You'll need to use an electric mixer to make this loaf, as it's important to emulsify the eggs, sugar, and oil almost to a mayonnaise-like consistency before adding the dry ingredients.

Ingredients

3 cups all-purpose flour
1 teaspoon baking soda
½ teaspoon baking powder
2 teaspoons ground cinnamon
¼ teaspoon ground allspice
½ teaspoon ground ginger
½ teaspoon salt

3 eggs
1¾ cups granulated sugar
1 cup sunflower oil
½ teaspoon vanilla extract
2 cups grated zucchini
¼ cup poppy seeds
1 tablespoon grated lemon zest

Method

Preheat the oven to 350°F. Butter and flour two 9 x 5-inch, 3-inch deep loaf pans.

Sift the flour, baking soda, baking powder, spices, and salt into a large bowl. In a separate bowl, beat the eggs with the sugar, using an electric mixer, until the mixture holds a ribbon-like trail on the surface. Add the oil in a slow stream, beating constantly until well incorporated. The mixture should have the consistency of mayonnaise. Add the vanilla, zucchini, poppy seeds, and lemon zest. Gently fold in the sifted dry ingredients.

Pour the batter into the prepared pans. Bake for 40–45 minutes, or until the loaf springs back slightly when gently pressed in the center. A wooden skewer inserted into the center should come out clean. Leave to cool in the pans for 5 minutes before turning out onto a wire rack. Allow to cool completely before serving.

Makes 2 large loaves

Pumpkin gingerbread

A bit of America and a bit of England are blended together in this loaf. The pumpkin makes it moist and adds depth to the flavor. The bread is best made the day before as the flavors will mellow overnight. Serve with butter or cream cheese.

Ingredients

2 cups all-purpose flour
½ teaspoon baking soda
1½ teaspoons ground ginger
½ teaspoon ground cinnamon
¼ teaspoon ground allspice
¼ teaspoon ground cloves
¼ teaspoon grated nutmeg

1 egg
½ cup granulated sugar
½ cup sunflower oil
½ cup canned pumpkin
1¼ cups molasses
⅓ cup stem ginger, drained, and cut into small dice

Method

Preheat the oven to 350°F. Butter and flour a 9-inch square cake pan.

Sift the flour, baking soda, and spices into a large bowl. In a separate bowl, beat the egg with the sugar, using an electric mixer, until pale and fluffy. Add the oil in a steady stream and beat until well incorporated. The mixture should have the consistency of mayonnaise. Add the pumpkin, molasses, and diced ginger. Add the sifted dry ingredients alternately with ½ cup hot water. Don't overmix.

Pour the batter into the prepared pan. Bake for 30–40 minutes, or until a wooden skewer inserted into the center comes out clean. Leave to cool in the pan for 5 minutes before turning out onto a wire rack. Allow to cool completely before serving.

Makes 1 large loaf

Corn bread

This American classic is a favorite in our household for breakfast, lunch, or dinner. It's moist and buttery, and really easy to make. Any leftovers can be sliced up and grilled on a hot pan or griddle. Serve with lots of fresh butter.

Ingredients

⅓ cup unsalted butter, melted and cooled
½ cup all-purpose flour
1½ cups cornmeal
1 teaspoon salt
1 teaspoon granulated sugar

1 tablespoon baking powder
2 eggs, well beaten
1¼ cups milk
¼ cup plain yogurt

Method

Preheat the oven to 500°F or its hottest setting.

Lightly grease a 9-inch square cake pan with some of the melted butter.

Sift the flour, cornmeal, salt, sugar, and baking powder into a large bowl. Make a well in the center. Add the eggs, milk, and yogurt. Stir in the remaining melted butter and mix until just combined.

Pour the batter into the prepared pan. Bake for 15 minutes, or until a wooden skewer inserted into the center comes out clean. Leave to cool in the pan for 2–3 minutes, then cut into squares. Serve immediately.

Makes 1 large loaf

Savory pumpkin bread

This unusual bread works very well as a base for a variety of open-faced sandwiches. It's dense and moist, and not dissimilar in texture to Irish potato bread. Cut the bread into squares, split them in half, and top with smoked salmon and crème fraîche, or Boursin and Apricot and cherry chutney (see page 141).

To prepare the pumpkin purée, cut a medium pumpkin into large chunks, leaving the skin on. Scoop out the seeds and fibers. Brush the flesh with a little olive oil, then roast in a preheated oven at 425°F for 30 minutes until tender. Scoop out the flesh and whiz in a food processor until smooth.

Ingredients

⅓ cup unsalted butter, melted and cooled
1¾ cups all-purpose flour
2 teaspoons baking powder
½ teaspoon baking soda
1 teaspoon salt
¼ teaspoon ground pepper

½ teaspoon paprika
¼ teaspoon cayenne pepper
2 eggs
1 cup fresh pumpkin purée (see above) or canned pumpkin
¾ cup buttermilk or plain yogurt

Method

Preheat the oven to 350°F.

Lightly grease a 9-inch square cake pan with some of the melted butter.

Sift the flour, baking powder, baking soda, salt, and spices into a large bowl. In a separate bowl, whisk the eggs until pale and fluffy. Add the pumpkin purée and the buttermilk to the eggs. Fold in the flour and spice mixture. Stir in the remaining melted butter.

Pour the batter into the prepared pan. Bake for 30–40 minutes, or until a wooden skewer inserted into the center comes out clean. Leave to cool in the pan for 5 minutes before turning out onto a wire racking. Allow to cool completely before serving.

Makes 1 large loaf

Pastry • Pumpkin pie • Apple pie • Coconut cream pie • Lemon meringue pie • Banana cream pie • Key lime pie • Crumb crust • Pecan pie Marc's rum-flavored whipped cream

Pies and strudels

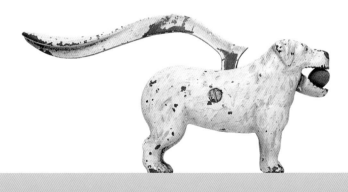

Holiday pie • Apple strudel • Banana strudel • Perfect whipped cream
Easy vanilla-bean custard • Perfect coffee • Marc's 45-minute espresso

My first real crush on a boy was when I was 11 years old. I wanted desperately to impress him, so I asked my mother if I could invite him for dinner. I volunteered to make a pie for dessert.

I selected a black bottom pie as my tool of seduction. It was a good choice, but unfortunately it was well beyond my capabilities. First I burned the chocolate custard filling. I then tried to mask the bitterness by adding loads of Cool Whip. It looked great but tasted horrible. My mother dished up the pie, and I watched with amazement as he ate the entire slice without even wincing. At first I thought he ate it because he loved me. But a few weeks later, I found out that he just didn't have any tastebuds.

My piemaking skills have come a long way since then – like anything else, practice makes perfect. To show off your homemade pie, choose an accompaniment that complements the filling. Serve the pie with some fabulous ice cream, homemade custard, or Perfect whipped cream (see page 80) and a really good cup of coffee.

✳ Tips for making perfect pies:

There are two clear rules when it comes to pies:

1 Don't make the pastry too thick or it will take over the whole pie. I prefer a thin, crisp, flaky crust with lots of filling.

2 Use the best fruit and ingredients for the filling. Don't attempt to get rid of overripe fruit or old bits and pieces by disguising them under pastry. It won't work.

Pastry

I use this all-purpose pastry for most pies, tarts, and quiches. It has a nice flaky, short crumb. Normally I am a staunch hater of margarine and cannot bear the sight of it, but this recipe is the one exception. I use a brand of kosher margarine called Tomar. It gives the pastry just the right amount of flakiness and the flavor is excellent. If you can't find Tomar margarine, then use a good-quality unsalted butter instead.

Ingredients

2 cups all-purpose flour
1 teaspoon salt

⅔ cup Tomar margarine (or unsalted butter)
¼ cup very cold water

Method

Sift the flour and salt into a large bowl. Cut up the margarine or butter into 1-inch chunks. If you have a food processor, place the flour and margarine in the processor and whiz for a few seconds until the mixture resembles coarse bread crumbs. Tip the contents of the food processor back into the large bowl. If making the pastry by hand, add the chunks of margarine or butter to the flour and rub in, using your fingertips, until the mixture looks like coarse bread crumbs.

Drizzle the cold water over the mixture and gently bring together to form a soft dough. Knead very gently, then form into a flat disk. Cover with plastic wrap and chill for 20 minutes.

Remove the dough from the fridge. On a very lightly floured surface, roll out the dough to about ⅛ inch thick. Lay the dough over the pan and gently coax it in, being careful to avoid stretching and tearing. Cut around the outside edge of the pan and flute the pastry edge as required. Leave the pie shell to rest in the fridge for 20 minutes. (This will help to prevent the pastry from shrinking too much during baking.) Any leftover scraps of dough can be gently rolled together and used for lattice tops or decorative touches.

To bake blind, preheat the oven to 425°F. Line the pie shell with a circle of parchment paper. Use ceramic baking beans or dried pulses to weigh down the paper. Bake for 8–12 minutes, or until the pastry has lost its raw color. Remove the beans and paper, and bake for a further 4–6 minutes, or until very lightly golden.

Makes two 9-inch pie shells

 Tips for making perfect pastry:

1 Use cold fat (margarine or butter), straight from the fridge.

2 Use very cold water and add by hand, not in the food processor.

3 Use as little water as possible to hold the dough together.

4 Don't overmix or over-handle the dough, or the pastry will be tough.

Pumpkin pie

I've converted even profound pumpkin haters with this pie. The filling is soft, silky, and almost custard-like, with lots of warm autumnal spices. At our first Thanksgiving in Silchester, I invited several of our new neighbors. They looked a bit frightened when I told them what the pie was, but once the first mouthfuls were swallowed, there were broad smiles all round. Scuffles broke out when the last slice was offered. It was a big success.

Ingredients

½ recipe all-purpose pastry (see page 65)
3 eggs
2 cups canned puréed pumpkin
1 cup light brown sugar, tightly packed
¼ teaspoon salt
1 teaspoon ground cinnamon

1 teaspoon grated nutmeg
½ teaspoon ground ginger
¼ teaspoon ground cloves
2 tablespoons bourbon
1½ cups evaporated milk

Method

Preheat the oven to 425°F.

Roll out the pastry dough to less than ⅛ inch thick and use to line a 9-inch round, 2-inch deep pie dish. Chill for 30 minutes. Meanwhile, beat the eggs in a bowl. Add the pumpkin, brown sugar, salt, spices, bourbon, and evaporated milk. Combine well.

Set the pie shell on a baking sheet and place on a partially pulled-out oven rack. Pour the filling into the pie shell, filling as high as you dare go. Gently slide into the oven. Bake for 15 minutes, then reduce the oven temperature to 325°F and bake for a further 25–30 minutes, or until the filling is just set. A knife inserted in the center of the pie should come out clean. Allow to cool completely before serving with Marc's rum-flavored whipped cream (see page 80).

Serves 6–8

Apple pie

Apple pie is comfort food at its most delicious. The smell of pastry, apples, and cinnamon wafting from the kitchen evokes happy memories for most people. This is a real "grandmother-style" pie – unfussy, uncomplicated and very yummy. Peter Robinson, a good friend and The Little Red Barn's first bookkeeper, once paid me the highest compliment ever. I invited him to Sunday lunch to thank him for all the hard work he had done on my behalf. After lunch, I served him a slice of apple pie. He looked up over his glasses and said: "I haven't had a pie this good since Great Granny Robinson's." And this was from a man who knew his pies! So in tribute to Peter, this recipe is dedicated to him.

Ingredients

5 cups apples (such as Macintosh), peeled, cored and sliced into ¼-inch chunks

Lemon juice

2 tablespoons all-purpose flour

½ cup granulated sugar

1 teaspoon ground cinnamon

½ teaspoon ground cloves

¼ teaspoon grated nutmeg

¼ teaspoon ground allspice

¼ teaspoon ground ginger

⅛ teaspoon salt

1 recipe all-purpose pastry (see page 65)

2–4 tablespoons unsalted butter, cut into small pieces

1 tablespoon milk

Raw sugar, for sprinkling

Method

Preheat the oven to 400°F.

Place the apples in a large bowl and sprinkle with a little lemon juice to stop them discoloring. Add the flour, sugar, spices, and salt, and stir gently to combine.

Roll out the pastry to a roundish shape about ⅛ inch thick. Place on a large baking sheet. Pile the apple mixture in the center of the pastry and dot with the butter. Gather up the pastry round the filling to form a rustic tart. The filling should be almost completely enclosed by the pastry. Brush the edges of the pastry round with a little milk and sprinkle with raw sugar.

Bake for 15 minutes, then reduce the oven temperature to 350°F and bake for a further 30 minutes, or until the apples are tender. Leave to rest for 10 minutes before serving.

Serves 6–8

Coconut cream pie

This is my interpretation of a classic diner pie. A warning, though: it's seriously decadent. The filling is fluffy and light, and it feels like you're eating a coconut cloud.

Ingredients

2⅔ cups sweetened shredded coconut

3 cups milk

1 envelope unflavored gelatin

½ cup granulated sugar

¼ cup cornstarch

1 egg

3 egg yolks

2 tablespoons unsalted butter

1 tablespoon vanilla extract

⅛ teaspoon salt

1 cup heavy cream

10-inch pre-baked pie shell, made with all-purpose pastry (see page 65)

Method

Preheat the oven to 350°F.

Spread half of the coconut on a baking sheet and toast in the oven for 8–10 minutes, or until lightly golden. Meanwhile, put ⅓ cup of the milk in a small bowl and sprinkle the gelatin on top. Leave to stand for 5 minutes.

Whisk the sugar, cornstarch, egg, and egg yolks together in a bowl. Pour the rest of the milk into a saucepan and bring almost to a boil. Gradually whisk the hot milk into the egg mixture. Add the softened gelatin, and pour into a clean saucepan. Cook over a gentle heat, stirring constantly, until the mixture is thick enough to just coat the back of a wooden spoon. Don't let it boil.

Remove from the heat and strain the mixture into a large metal bowl. Stir in the butter, vanilla, salt, and untoasted coconut.

Set the bowl in a basin of cold water and stir occasionally until the custard reaches setting point. This means when you draw a spoon through the middle you will see the bottom of the bowl.

Working quickly, whip the cream until it holds soft peaks. Gently fold into the coconut custard using the minimum amount of strokes. Pour the filling into the pie shell and chill for about 4 hours, or until set. Just before serving, sprinkle the toasted coconut on top.

Serves 6–8

Lemon meringue pie

A pie classic, the lemon meringue pie has been much abused over the years. This recipe brings you back to good old basics. You will re-discover what a dynamite flavor and texture sensation this pie has. The crisp meringue top dissolves into a fluffy cloud-like underlayer. Then the tangy lemon filling kicks in along with the snap of flaky pastry. If you want a really, really decadent experience, serve this with some Easy vanilla-bean custard (see page 80), or with cream.

For the filling

1 cup granulated sugar
3 tablespoons all-purpose flour
3 tablespoons cornstarch
¼ teaspoon salt

3 egg yolks
1 tablespoon grated lemon zest
⅓ cup fresh lemon juice
2 tablespoons unsalted butter

For the meringue

3 egg whites, at room temperature
½ cup + 2 tablespoons superfine sugar
1 cup + 2 tablespoons confectioners' sugar

9-inch pre-baked pie shell, made with all-purpose pastry (see page 65)

Method

To make the filling, mix ½ cup of the sugar with the flour, cornstarch, and salt in a double boiler or bowl set over a pan of hot water. Stir in 1½ cups boiling water. Cook over a low heat, stirring, until the mixture thickens and begins to boil.

In a bowl, combine the egg yolks with the remaining sugar. Slowly add to the hot sugar and flour mixture. Continue stirring over a low heat until the mixture thickens. You should be able to draw a spoon through the middle and see the bottom of the bowl. This can take up to 20 minutes. Don't let the mixture boil. Remove from the heat, add the lemon zest and juice, and the butter. Stir. Leave the mixture to cool to lukewarm, then pour into the pie shell. Preheat the oven to 250°F.

To prepare the meringue, beat the egg whites until soft peaks form. Add the superfine sugar, little by little, whisking well after each addition. The egg whites should be very stiff and shiny. Sift the confectioners' sugar over the egg whites and carefully fold in, using a large metal spoon, using the minimum number of strokes, until the confectioners' sugar is well distributed.

Pile the meringue on top of the lemon filling, making sure the filling is well covered. Bake for 1 hour. The meringue should be light and dry, with a creamy center.

Serves 6–8

Banana cream pie

This is a special treat for banana-lovers. it's easy to make, delicious and children love it.

Ingredients

3 cups whole milk
1 envelope unflavored gelatin
½ cup granulated sugar
¼ cup cornstarch
1 egg
3 egg yolks
2 tablespoons unsalted butter

1 teaspoon vanilla extract
⅛ teaspoon salt
2–3 medium firm, ripe bananas
9-inch pre-baked pie shell, made with crumb crust (see page 73) or all-purpose pastry (see page 65)
½ cup Perfect whipped cream (see page 80)

Method

Pour ⅓ cup of the milk into a small bowl. Sprinkle the gelatin on top of the milk. Leave to stand for 5 minutes, stirring gently to dissolve the grains.

In a separate bowl, whisk the sugar, cornstarch, egg, and egg yolks. Pour the remaining milk into a saucepan and bring almost to a boil. Gradually whisk the hot milk into the egg and sugar mixture. Add the milk and gelatin mixture and pour into a clean saucepan. Cook over a gentle heat, stirring constantly, until the mixture is thick enough to just coat the back of a spoon. Don't allow it to boil.

Remove from the heat and strain the mixture into a bowl. Stir in the butter, vanilla, and salt.

Cut the bananas into ¼-inch chunks and add to the custard. Gently mix through. Leave the custard to cool for 10 minutes before pouring into the pre-baked pie shell. Chill for at least 2 hours before serving. Just before serving, prepare the Perfect whipped cream (see page 80). Spoon or pipe the cream over the pie and serve immediately.

Serves 6–8

★ Note: The key to this recipe is using bananas which are just ripe, full of banana flavor, but still firm.

Key lime pie

This is a very refreshing pie that is quick to make – it has all the charm of a lemon meringue pie with a third of the fuss. Note that it contains raw eggs.

Ingredients

Finely grated zest of 1 lime
Juice of 2 limes
Juice of 1 lemon
1¾ cups condensed milk

3 egg yolks
⅛ teaspoon salt
9-inch pre-baked pie shell, made
with crumb crust (see below)

Method

Combine the lime zest and juice, and lemon juice in a bowl. Add the condensed milk, egg yolks, and salt. Whisk to blend all the ingredients.

Pour the filling into the pie shell and chill for at least 2 hours before serving. Serve on its own or with a fresh raspberry sauce.

Serves 6–8

Crumb crust

Most cookies work well, but I think graham crackers make the best crumb crust. Make the crumbs in a food processor or by putting the cookies or crackers in a polythene bag and crushing with a rolling pin.

Ingredients

⅔ cup blanched almonds
¼ cup granulated sugar

1 cup cookie or graham cracker crumbs
½ cup (1 stick) unsalted butter, melted

Method

Preheat the oven to 350°F.

Place the almonds on a baking sheet and toast in the oven for 10 minutes until fragrant. Allow to cool, then grind finely in a food processor. Mix the ground almonds, sugar, and cookie or graham cracker crumbs in a large bowl. Add the melted butter and stir with a fork to combine. Press the mixture onto the bottom and sides of a 9-inch pie plate or springform cake pan. Bake for 10 minutes, or until lightly browned.

Makes a 9-inch pie shell

Pecan pie

I make this Thanksgiving classic all year round. It's easy to prepare and the flavor is intense. Despite what all other recipe books tell you, you can't make a good pecan pie without Karo corn syrup.

Ingredients

9-inch uncooked pie shell, made with all-purpose pastry (see page 65)

1 cup pecan halves

2 eggs

1 cup light corn syrup

½ cup dark brown sugar, tightly packed

1 teaspoon vanilla extract

1 tablespoon bourbon

¼ teaspoon salt

¼ cup unsalted butter, cut into small pieces

Method

Preheat the oven to 425°F.

Line the bottom of the pie shell with the pecan halves, placing them in a decorative pattern. Beat the eggs in a large bowl. Add the corn syrup, brown sugar, vanilla, bourbon, and salt. Blend well. Pour this mixture over the pecans, and dot with butter.

Bake for 10 minutes, then reduce the oven temperature to 325°F and bake for a further 30 minutes, or until the filling is just firm in the center. Leave to cool, in the pan, on a wire rack. Serve warm with Marc's rum-flavored whipped cream (see below).

Serves 6–8

Marc's rum-flavored whipped cream

Use a good dark rum. If you can't get a good dark drinking rum, use a good Cognac. Remember, the flavor of raw alcohol can be quite strong, so don't use anything you wouldn't be happy drinking on its own. You'll only need a little bit, so even if you use something expensive, the flavor will be well worth it.

Ingredients

1 cup whipping cream, well chilled

1 tablespoon dark rum (Cognac or brandy)

2 tablespoons granulated sugar

Method

Follow the method given for Perfect whipped cream (see page 80), but combine the cream and the rum before adding the sugar.

Holiday pie

The mix of fresh and dried fruit in this pie is delicious. It's really a light version of a traditional mince pie, with all the wonderful spices and aroma of Christmas. Serve this with Marc's rum-flavored whipped cream (see page 75), and you'll be hearing those sleigh bells ring!

Ingredients

1 recipe all-purpose pastry (see page 65)
1 medium apple (such as Macintosh), peeled, cored and diced
1 medium ripe banana, peeled and diced
¼ cup unsalted butter, melted
½ cup golden raisins
⅔ cup currants
¼ cup chopped mixed candied peel

¼ cup chopped unblanched almonds
Grated zest of 1 lemon
½ teaspoon ground cinnamon
¼ teaspoon grated nutmeg
¼ teaspoon ground cloves
¼ teaspoon ground allspice
1 tablespoon rum (Cognac or sherry)
⅓ cup light brown sugar, tightly packed

Method

Preheat the oven to 425°F.

Roll out the pastry dough to less than ⅛ inch thick and use to line a 9-inch pie pan. Reserve the pastry trimmings. Bake blind for 20 minutes (see page 65), or until the pastry has just lost its raw look and is slightly golden. Remove from the oven and set aside. Reduce the oven temperature to 375°F.

To prepare the filling, place the apple in a large bowl. Add the banana together with the butter, raisins, currants, candied peel, almonds, lemon zest, spices, rum, and sugar. Mix to combine. Spoon the filling evenly into the pie shell. Using the reserved pastry trimmings, roll out several strips to form a lattice on top of the pie, arranging them to make a diamond pattern. Brush the lattice with water and sprinkle with a little extra sugar. Bake for 10–15 minutes, or until the pastry is golden and the filling is cooked.

Serves 6–8

Apple strudel

This classic strudel makes a great last-minute dessert. Serve with either ice cream or a little Perfect whipped cream (see page 80).

Ingredients

4 medium apples (such as Macintosh), peeled, cored and diced

⅓ cup golden raisins

¼ cup light brown sugar, tightly packed

1 teaspoon ground cinnamon

¼ teaspoon salt

1 tablespoon grated lemon zest

4 sheets of frozen filo pastry, thawed

½ cup (1 stick) unsalted butter, melted

¼ cup pecans, toasted and coarsely chopped

1 cup fresh bread crumbs

Granulated sugar, for sprinkling

Method

Preheat the oven to 400°F.

Mix together the apples, raisins, brown sugar, cinnamon, salt, and lemon zest. Set aside.

Stack and trim the sheets of filo pastry to a 15 x 12-inch rectangle. Peel off one sheet and brush with melted butter. Place a second sheet on top and brush it with butter. Repeat with the remaining two sheets, brushing each sheet with butter.

Spread the fruit filling over the top layer of pastry, leaving a clear 1-inch border along all the edges. Sprinkle the filling with the toasted pecans and bread crumbs. Roll up the pastry like a jelly roll, starting from one long side. Seal all the edges, brushing them with butter to hold them in place, and tucking the side edges under. Place the roll seam-side down on a baking sheet and brush with the last of the butter. Sprinkle with granulated sugar.

Bake for 10–15 minutes, or until crisp and golden. Serve warm.

Serves 6–8

★ Note: This strudel reheats very well. Place it on a baking sheet and bake in a preheated 350°F oven for 8–10 minutes.

Banana strudel

This banana strudel recipe came from an impromptu evening, when I literally made the dessert as my guests were chatting away in the garden. Be sure to use a ripe but firm banana.

Ingredients

⅓ cup golden raisins

2 tablespoons rum

1 medium ripe banana, diced

1½ tablespoons light brown sugar, tightly packed

½ teaspoon grated nutmeg

⅛ teaspoon salt

⅓ cup unsalted butter, melted

4 sheets of frozen filo pastry, thawed

½ cup lightly toasted bread crumbs

Granulated sugar, for sprinkling

Method

Preheat the oven to 400°F.

Soak the raisins in the rum in a bowl for a few minutes. Add the diced banana, brown sugar, nutmeg, salt, and 1 tablespoon of the melted butter. Set aside.

Stack and trim the sheets of filo pastry to a 15 x 12-inch rectangle. Peel off one sheet and brush with melted butter. Place a second sheet on top and brush with butter. Repeat with the remaining two sheets, brushing each sheet with butter.

Spread the fruit filling over the top layer of pastry, leaving a clear 1-inch border along all the edges. Sprinkle the filling with the toasted bread crumbs. Roll up the pastry like a jelly roll, starting from one long side. Seal all the edges, brushing them with butter to hold them in place, and tucking the side edges under. Place the roll seam-side down on a baking sheet and brush with the last of the butter. Sprinkle with granulated sugar.

Bake for 10–15 minutes, or until crisp and golden. Serve warm.

Serves 4–6

Perfect whipped cream

Ingredients

1 cup whipping cream, well chilled
2 tablespoons granulated sugar

Method

If you have time, chill the mixing bowl and beaters or whisk in the freezer for 10–15 minutes. Put the cream and sugar into the bowl. With an electric mixer, start whipping on a slow speed and gently increase to high. The cream is ready when it just starts to form very soft peaks and just about holds its shape. Any more than this and you've overdone it. Because an electric mixer can be a bit ferocious, it's best to switch over to a hand whisk just before the cream is ready. If you feel vigorous and energetic, you can do it all by hand. Use a nice big balloon whisk. It won't take long and you'll get the best results.

Serves 4–6

Easy vanilla-bean custard

Custard is one of those things you either really love or hate. I can't imagine anyone not liking this. It's totally seductive. You'll want to have it day in and day out. Use fresh eggs, whole milk and a real vanilla bean for the best flavor.

Ingredients

2 cups whole milk
1 vanilla bean
3 egg yolks
⅓ cup granulated sugar

1 tablespoon all-purpose flour
1 tablespoon cornstarch
1 tablespoon unsalted butter

Method

Heat the milk with the vanilla bean in a saucepan until it almost comes to a boil. Remove from the heat and leave the milk to infuse for 15 minutes. Remove the vanilla bean, split it in half, and scrape out the seeds. Add the seeds to the milk and discard the bean. Heat gently until the milk is hot again. Whisk together the egg yolks, sugar, flour, and cornstarch in a small bowl. Add the hot milk to the egg yolk mixture. Pour this into a clean saucepan and stir constantly over a low heat until the mixture thickens. This can take up to 15 minutes. Don't allow it to boil, as this can cause the custard to separate. The custard is ready when you draw a spoon through it and you can see the bottom of the pan. Spoon the custard into a clean bowl, add the butter and gently mix to incorporate. Serve warm or allow to cool. Cover and keep in the fridge for up to 48 hours.

Serves 4–6

Perfect coffee

It may seem like an arrogant thing to say, but not many people can make a really good cup of coffee. Having been born in Colombia, I can safely say that coffee runs through my veins, and I'm picky about what I drink.

To make the perfect cup of coffee you need to start with some good beans. The freshness of the beans is critical. You also need to be patient. For best results buy beans and grind them yourself. Electric coffee grinders are readily available and they're not expensive. It's the one kitchen gadget you'll use every day, so it's worth the small investment and the space it will take up on your work surface or in your cupboard.

Just so you recognize a great cup of coffee when you taste one, here's a short description. The coffee should be piping hot with an unmistakably fresh coffee aroma. The perfect flavor is akin to that of a fine wine, where the balance of body, flavor and acidity are in total harmony. The perfect cup will be full-bodied and smooth, with a clean coffee taste. There should be no trace of bitterness, which comes from over-roasting or rushing the process. Don't confuse bitterness with acidity. Acidity helps define the flavor. Some coffees are higher in acidity than others and that really does come down to personal taste.

Here's how to make a great cup of filtered coffee.

Ingredients

Coffee beans
Fresh water

Method

Grind the beans very finely. Fit the paper filter into the cone and set over the pitcher. Fill with the amount of coffee required – a good heaping tablespoon per cup. Bring the water to a boil. Let it sit for a minute or two, then pour enough water over the coffee grinds just to moisten them. Allow it to stand for at least a minute. This helps to release the flavor of the beans. Then slowly add a bit more water, a little at a time. Don't rush it. Let the water seep through the beans gently before adding more water. The whole process should take 4–5 minutes. Drink up!

Marc's 45-minute espresso

The 45-minute espresso was born in July, 1998, in a lovely, primitive farmhouse on the borders of Umbria and Tuscany, where the horses slept on the ground floor and we all slept on the first floor. Undoubtedly, the special location did help the flavor of the espresso, but we still enjoy it at home. In today's rushed world there is something very therapeutic about waiting 45 minutes for anything.

Ingredients

Freshly ground espresso coffee
Fresh mineral water

Method

Take one of those classic aluminum espresso coffee pots and densely pack the container with freshly ground espresso coffee. Use a tool that will allow you to pack the coffee in tightly. Use mineral water to fill up the water chamber, and screw all of the components together very tightly. Now comes the tricky part. Set the pot over the smallest flame possible (hopefully you'll have access to a gas range for this). In Italy, we called that tiny flame "the flame of love." Now leave the gentle heat to do its bit, and retire to read the newspaper or have a siesta. Forty-five minutes later you will hear a throaty gurgle and then smell the aroma of freshly made coffee. Serve in white porcelain espresso cups, perhaps with slice of moist Lemon tea bread (see page 54).

Brownies

Rum and raisin brownies • Peanut butter brownies • Raspberry and almond brownies • Cheesecake swirl brownies

I'm sure those of you who have tasted The Little Red Barn brownies have turned to this chapter first of all. So many of our customers and friends have requested our special brownie recipe that I promised to include a few in the book, even if it meant giving away a secret or two.

The nice thing about brownies is that most people love them, young and old alike. There's nothing more wonderful than a slightly warm, very chocolatey brownie. For me, the best brownies are full of chocolate, very squidgy and gooey in the middle, but slightly chewy and crispy on top. The edges and corner pieces are my favorite bits.

Brownies are great at any time of the day or night, and they can be dressed up or down depending on the circumstances. I sometimes cut them into small pieces and serve them as petits fours at the end of a dinner party. They're also great in lunch boxes and perfect for picnics.

✹ Tips for making great brownies:

1 Don't overmix. You don't want lots of air in the mixture.

2 Bake in a square pan. I don't know why, but they always taste better.

3 Don't overbake. This is where most people go wrong.

The Little Red Barn

Rum and raisin brownies

Rum, raisins, and chocolate are a such a good combination. These brownies are best made the day before you want to serve them as the flavor of the rum will develop and mellow overnight. For the ultimate brownie experience, serve these brownies slightly warm, topped with a dollop of mascarpone.

Ingredients

¾ cup golden raisins

⅓ cup dark rum

1 cup all-purpose flour

¼ teaspoon salt

4 ounces semisweet chocolate

½ cup (1 stick) unsalted butter

¾ cup dark brown sugar, tightly packed

¾ cup granulated sugar

2 eggs

Method

Soak the raisins in the rum for at least 30 minutes, but preferably overnight.

Preheat the oven to 325°F. Butter and flour a 9-inch square cake pan.

Sift the flour and salt into a large bowl. Melt the chocolate with the butter in a double boiler or bowl set over a pan of hot water (or you can use a microwave). Add the brown and granulated sugars and leave to dissolve slightly, then stir to combine. Add the eggs, one by one, beating after each addition. The mixture should be very glossy. Add the raisins and rum. Gently fold in the flour. Don't overmix.

Spread the batter in the prepared pan to form an even layer. Bake for 20–25 minutes, or until just set in the middle. A wooden skewer inserted into the center should come out with just a few moist crumbs on it. Don't overbake. Leave to cool completely in the pan before cutting into squares and serving.

Makes 16–20 brownies

★ Note: If you prefer a plain Double Chocolate brownie leave out the rum and raisins. Add an extra 4 ounces semisweet chocolate chunks to the flour together with 1 teaspoon vanilla extract.

Peanut butter brownies

Peanut butter with chocolate is a classic flavor combination. I think this is a stunning brownie, beautifully layered and tasting full on of peanuts and chocolate. Use unsweetened peanut butter if available.

Ingredients

4 ounces semisweet chocolate

½ cup (1 stick) unsalted butter

⅔ cup all-purpose flour

½ teaspoon baking powder

½ teaspoon salt

¾ cup granulated sugar

½ cup light brown sugar, tightly packed

2 eggs

1 teaspoon vanilla extract

½ cup crunchy peanut butter

Method

Preheat the oven to 350°F. Butter and flour a 9-inch square cake pan.

Melt the chocolate with half of the butter in a double boiler or bowl set over a pan of hot water (or you can use a microwave). Stir to combine, then leave to cool for a few minutes. Meanwhile, sift the flour, baking powder, and salt into a large bowl.

In a separate bowl, beat the remaining butter with the granulated and brown sugars until pale and fluffy. Add the eggs, one by one, beating after each addition. The mixture should have the consistency of mayonnaise. Add the vanilla. Gently fold in the flour. Don't overmix.

Spoon half of the batter into another bowl. To one half add the peanut butter, and to the other half add the melted chocolate. Spread the peanut butter batter in the prepared pan to form an even layer. Spread the chocolate batter evenly over the top. Bake for 20–25 minutes, or until set in the middle. A wooden skewer inserted into the center should come out with just a few moist crumbs on it. Don't overbake. Leave to cool completely in the pan before cutting into squares and serving.

Makes 16–20 brownies

Raspberry and almond brownies

The combination of fresh raspberries, toasted almonds, and chocolate makes these brownies very luxurious. Serve them warm out of the oven, with ice cream or in a pool of Easy vanilla-bean custard (see page 80).

Ingredients

1 cup all-purpose flour
½ teaspoon salt
4 ounces semisweet chocolate
½ cup (1 stick) unsalted butter
¾ cup dark brown sugar, tightly packed

¾ cup granulated sugar
2 eggs
1 generous cup fresh raspberries
½ cup sliced almonds

Method

Preheat the oven to 325°F. Butter and flour a 9-inch square cake pan.

Sift the flour and salt into a large bowl. Melt the chocolate with the butter in a double boiler or a bowl set over a pan of hot water (or you can use a microwave). Remove from the heat, add the brown and granulated sugars and leave to dissolve slightly, then stir to combine. Add the eggs, one by one, beating after each addition. The mixture should be very glossy. Gently fold in the flour. Don't overmix.

Spread the batter in the prepared pan to form an even layer. Top with the raspberries and sliced almonds. Bake for 20–30 minutes, or until just set in the middle. A wooden skewer inserted into the center should come out with just a few moist crumbs on it. Don't overbake. Leave to cool in the pan for 30 minutes before cutting into squares and serving.

Makes 16–20 brownies

Cheesecake swirl brownies

I think you'll appreciate the simplicity and elegance of this brownie. The combination of cheesecake and chocolate brownie is surprisingly light.

For the chocolate mixture

4 ounces semisweet chocolate
½ cup (1 stick) unsalted butter
¾ cup granulated sugar
2 eggs
½ cup all-purpose flour
¼ teaspoon salt

For the cheesecake mixture

1 cup cream cheese
¼ cup granulated sugar
½ teaspoon vanilla extract
1 egg

Method

Preheat the oven to 300°F. Butter and flour a 9-inch square cake pan.

To make the chocolate mixture, melt the chocolate with the butter in a double boiler or a bowl set over a pan of hot water (or you can use a microwave). Remove from the heat, add the sugar and stir to combine, then leave to cool slightly. Sift the flour and salt into a large bowl. Add the eggs, one by one, beating after each addition. The mixture should be very glossy. Gently fold in the flour. Don't overmix. Set aside.

To make the cheesecake mixture, beat the cream cheese with the sugar. Add the vanilla and egg, and mix until well combined.

Spread the chocolate batter in the prepared pan to form an even layer. Spoon the cheesecake mixture on top and spread evenly. Using a sharp knife, gently swirl the cheese mixture into the chocolate mixture a few times. Bake for 20–30 minutes, or until just set in the middle. A wooden skewer inserted into the center should come out with just a few moist crumbs on it. Don't overbake. Leave to cool in the pan for 15–20 minutes before cutting into squares and serving. Serve warm or cold.

Makes 16–20 brownies

Dalia's luscious lemon bars • Maple butter cookies • Polly's Mom's peanut cookies • Mrs J's molasses cookies

Cookies

Rolled sugar cookies • almond crunch bars • Chocolate truffle cookies • Toffee

It wasn't until I came to live in England that I discovered the joys of walking in the countryside. I was introduced to the post-lunch Sunday walk by my husband and mother-in-law. Being a city girl, I liked the idea, but was unsure about what exactly was involved. The only walking I had done previously was on city sidewalks. The idea of country walking seemed quaint, romantic, and wonderfully English.

They broke me in gently. At first it was all very civilized, with walks taking in the sights of Oxford and Blenheim Palace. They kept me along the fringes of the countryside and along proper paths. Then I progressed to narrow lanes, with the odd horse track here and there, and the occasional bit of mud that was easily side-stepped. Then I must have graduated, because on one particular walk in Rousham near Oxford, we encountered a river of mud such as I've never seen before. I was horrified to find that I was expected to walk the length of this, over a two-mile stretch, with my boots literally sinking into the ground. Not wanting to give a bad impression, I soldiered on, thinking the whole time of the delicious shortbread that would be waiting for us when we got home.

That's the nice thing about cookies. They're so easy to make. You can bake them days beforehand and have them sitting there waiting for you. I love coming back from a muddy walk, when it's been pouring with rain, kicking off my boots, and settling down in front of the television with a plate of home-baked cookies, sharing them with Marc and Oscar, my two best friends.

All you need to make a delicious batch of cookies is a mixing bowl, a large wooden spoon, and a little muscle power. You can produce a whole range of tastes and textures, from soft and crumbly oatmeal cookies to crunchy peanut cookies or tangy lemon bars. Keep them in airtight tins or put them in bags and store them in the freezer. They'll be there, waiting to help soothe away the stresses and strains of everyday life.

Dalia's luscious lemon bars

These cookie bars consist of a delicious shortbread base with a lemony topping and finished with a dusting of confectioners' sugar. If you can't be bothered to make a lemon meringue pie, then this is a very good alternative. Serve with fresh raspberries.

For the base

2 cups all-purpose flour
½ cup confectioners' sugar
1 cup (2 sticks) unsalted butter, cut into chunks

For the topping

4 eggs
2 cups granulated sugar
⅓ cup lemon juice
¼ cup all-purpose flour
½ teaspoon baking powder
Confectioners' sugar, for dusting

Method

Preheat the oven to 350°F. Lightly grease a 13 x 9-inch cake pan.

To make the base, sift the flour and confectioners' sugar into a large bowl. Rub the butter into the flour and sugar, using your fingertips, to make a soft dough.

Press the dough into the bottom of the prepared pan. Bake for 15–20 minutes, or until lightly golden.

Meanwhile, prepare the filling. Beat the eggs, sugar, and lemon juice together in a bowl. Stir in the flour and baking powder.

When the shortbread base is ready, remove from the oven and leave to cool for a few minutes. Pour the lemon filling over the shortbread base. Bake for a further 25 minutes, or until the filling is set. Leave to cool in the pan for several hours before dusting with confectioners' sugar, cutting into bars, and serving.

Makes 24–30 bars

Barbara's pecan dainties

I found this recipe amongst some old clippings my mother sent to me a few years ago. The moment I saw it, I was overtaken with nostalgia. I could remember exactly what these tasted like, and how I looked forward to them, whenever I saw them listed on her bridge luncheon menus.

Ingredients

½ cup (1 stick) unsalted butter
1 cup granulated sugar
1 egg, lightly beaten
1 tablespoon grated lemon zest
1 tablespoon lemon juice

2 cups all-purpose flour
1 teaspoon baking powder
⅛ teaspoon salt
1 cup finely chopped pecans

Method

Cream the butter with the sugar until pale and fluffy. Add the lightly beaten egg, lemon zest and juice, and mix well. Sift the flour, baking powder, and salt into a large bowl. Add the sifted dry ingredients and pecans to the butter and sugar mixture, and combine to make a stiff dough.

Turn the dough out onto a board and divide in half. Roll each half into a long sausage shape about 1½ inches in diameter. Wrap in parchment paper and chill for at least 1 hour.

Preheat the oven to 350°F. Lightly grease two baking sheets.

Using a sharp knife, slice each roll of dough across into ⅛-inch thick slices. Place the slices on the prepared baking sheets, allowing space for spreading. Bake for 8–10 minutes, or until lightly golden around the edges. Leave to cool on the baking sheets for a few minutes before transferring to a wire rack. Allow to cool completely before serving.

Makes 50–60 cookies

Maple butter cookies

These pretty cookies have a light maple flavor. Their crunchy texture is due to the use of bread flour instead of all-purpose flour. If you're into dunking, try these dunked in ice-cold milk, or with a latte. They're also nice served with ice cream.

Ingredients

3 cups strong flour

1 teaspoon salt

1 cup (2 sticks) unsalted butter

1 cup superfine sugar

½ cup maple syrup

1 egg

Method

Sift the flour and salt into a large bowl. In a separate bowl, cream the butter with the sugar until pale and fluffy. Add the maple syrup and egg, and mix well. Fold in the sifted dry ingredients and combine to make a stiff dough. Cover with plastic wrap and chill for 2 hours.

Preheat the oven to 350°F. Lightly grease two baking sheets.

Cut the dough in half. Roll out one half on a lightly floured surface to about ⅛ inch thick. Cut out leaf shapes using a maple leaf (or other leaf) cookie cutter. Place the cookies on the baking sheets. Roll out the rest of the dough and cut out as before. Gather up all the scraps, re-roll, and cut out more leaves. If the dough becomes too soft as you're working with it, chill it in the freezer for a few minutes.

Mark the cut-out cookies with foliage lines, using the back of a knife. Bake for 10–12 minutes, or until the edges are golden. Leave to cool on the baking sheets for a few minutes before transferring to a wire rack. Allow to cool completely before serving.

Makes 60 cookies

Snickerdoodles

The name of these cookies always makes me smile. They're really simple and unpretentious, and all the more delicious for it. Snickerdoodles have a soft cake-like texture and are just the sort of thing your Grandma would bake.

For the cookies

3 cups all-purpose flour
½ teaspoon salt
¾ teaspoon baking soda
1 teaspoon cream of tartar
1 cup (2 sticks) unsalted butter
1½ cups granulated sugar
1½ teaspoons vanilla extract
2 eggs
¼ cup milk

For the topping

3 tablespoons raw sugar
1 tablespoon granulated sugar
3 tablespoons ground cinnamon

Method

Preheat the oven to 375°F. Lightly grease two baking sheets.

Sift the flour, salt, baking soda, and cream of tartar into a large bowl. In a separate bowl, cream the butter with the sugar until pale and fluffy. Add the vanilla, eggs, and milk, and beat thoroughly. Fold in the sifted dry ingredients and combine to form a soft dough.

For the topping, combine all the ingredients in a small bowl.

Shape the dough into 1-inch balls. Dip one side of each ball in the topping mixture and place, topping-side up, on the prepared baking sheets, leaving space for spreading. Bake for 8–10 minutes, or until puffed up and lightly golden around the edges. Leave to cool for a few minutes on the baking sheets before transferring to wire racks. Allow to cool completely before serving.

Makes 30–40 cookies

Polly's Mom's peanut cookies

For years I've been searching for the perfect peanut cookies. This recipe, donated by Polly's Mom, hits the spot. The peanut flavor is perfect and the texture is crisp and delicate.

Ingredients

½ cup (1 stick) unsalted butter
½ cup light brown sugar, tightly packed
1 cup salted peanuts

4 teaspoons freshly brewed strong black coffee
1¼ cups self-rising flour
½ teaspoon ground cinnamon

Method

Preheat the oven to 350°F. Lightly grease two baking sheets.

Cream the butter with the sugar. Add the peanuts and black coffee, and stir to combine. Fold in the flour and cinnamon to make a soft dough. Pinch off pieces of dough the size of large marbles and roll into balls. Place on the prepared baking sheets, leaving space for spreading. Press down with a fork to flatten. Bake for 8–10 minutes, or until crisp and golden. Leave to cool for a few minutes on the baking sheets before transferring to a wire rack. Allow to cool completely before serving.

Makes 25 cookies

Ginger crisps

I like the contrast of sharp crystallized ginger with a very buttery cookie flavor.

Ingredients

1½ cups all-purpose flour
¾ teaspoon baking powder
½ teaspoon ground ginger
½ teaspoon salt
1 cup (2 sticks) unsalted butter

1 cup light brown sugar, tightly packed
1 egg
1 teaspoon vanilla extract
½ cup crystallized ginger, diced

Method

Preheat the oven to 350°F.

Sift the flour, baking powder, ginger, and salt into a large bowl. Cream the butter with the sugar until pale and fluffy. Add the egg and vanilla, and beat thoroughly. Add the crystallized ginger. Fold in the sifted dry ingredients. Drop tablespoonfuls of the dough onto ungreased baking sheets, leaving space for spreading. Bake for 10–12 minutes, or until just golden. Leave to cool on the baking sheets for 5 minutes before transferring to a wire rack. Allow to cool completely before serving.

Makes 50–60 cookies

Mrs J's molasses cookies

One of my best friends from high school was Mariella Jeanttet. Her mother made fantastic molasses cookies, and I loved going round to her house and eating these in the kitchen while we did our homework. The cookies are partly chewy, partly crunchy and have just the right amount of spiciness. Serve with glasses of ice-cold milk.

Ingredients

4 cups all-purpose flour
1 teaspoon baking soda
1 teaspoon salt
2 teaspoons ground cinnamon
1 teaspoon ground cloves
1 teaspoon ground ginger

1 cup (2 sticks) unsalted butter
2 cups granulated sugar
2 eggs
½ cup molasses
Raw sugar, for dipping

Method

Preheat the oven to 350°F. Lightly grease three baking sheets.

Sift the flour, baking soda, salt, and spices into a large bowl. In a separate bowl, cream the butter with the granulated sugar until pale and fluffy. Add the eggs and beat thoroughly. Add the molasses. Fold in the sifted dry ingredients to make a stiff dough.

Place some raw sugar in a small bowl. Pinch off pieces of dough the size of large marbles and roll into neat balls. Dip one side of the balls in the raw sugar and place, sugar-side up, on a prepared baking sheet, leaving space for spreading. Continue shaping balls until all the dough is used up. Bake for 10–12 minutes, or until golden. Leave to cool on the baking sheets for a few minutes before transferring to a wire rack. Allow to cool completely before serving.

Makes 80–90 cookies

 Note: These cookies freeze well. Make a batch and store them in plastic bags in the freezer. Leave to defrost for 1 hour before serving.

Rolled sugar cookies

I think these were the first cookies I ever made. Crisp and buttery, they're loved by adults and children alike. You can really have some fun with them, as they can be cut into different shapes and decorated to suit the occasion.

Ingredients

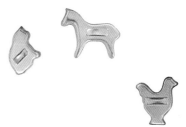

2 cups all-purpose flour
1½ teaspoons baking powder
½ teaspoon salt
½ cup unsalted butter
1 cup granulated sugar
1 egg, lightly beaten
1 teaspoon vanilla extract
1 tablespoon milk or cream
Tubes of ready-made writing icing, for decorating

Method

Sift the flour, baking powder, and salt into a large bowl. In a separate bowl, cream the butter with the sugar until pale and fluffy. Add the egg and beat well. Add the vanilla and milk or cream. Gently fold in the flour to make a stiff dough.

Divide the dough in half. Shape each half into a rectangle and flatten slightly with a rolling pin. Cover in plastic wrap and chill for at least 1 hour.

Preheat the oven to 375°F.

Roll out each rectangle of dough to about ⅛ inch thick. Stamp out the cookies with decorative cutters and place on ungreased baking sheets, leaving space for spreading. Bake for 8–10 minutes, or until lightly golden around the edges. Leave to cool on the baking sheets for a few minutes before transferring to a wire rack. Allow to cool completely before decorating with tubes of ready-made writing icing.

Makes 50–60 cookies

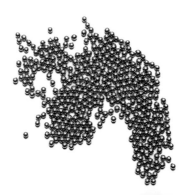

Soft and crumbly oatmeal cookies

If a luxurious weekend retreat is out of the question, here's an alternative. Curl up on the sofa, with a comforter wrapped round you, and tuck into a plate of these. They're humble and, dare I say, wholesome. Their texture is divine, soft and crumbly with little crisp edges.

Ingredients

1¾ cups large rolled oats
¾ cup all-purpose flour
1 teaspoon ground cinnamon
½ teaspoon baking soda
½ teaspoon salt

½ cup (1 stick) unsalted butter
⅓ cup light brown sugar, tightly packed
⅓ cup granulated sugar
1 egg

Method

Preheat the oven to 375°F. Lightly grease two baking sheets.

Combine the oats, flour, cinnamon, baking soda, and salt in a large bowl. Stir to mix through. In a separate bowl, cream the butter with the brown and granulated sugars until pale and fluffy. Add the egg and beat until well mixed. Fold in the oats and flour mixture.

Drop tablespoonfuls of the dough onto the prepared baking sheets, leaving space for spreading. Bake for 8–10 minutes, or until lightly golden around the edges. Leave to cool on the baking sheets for a few minutes before transferring to a wire rack. Allow to cool completely before serving.

Makes 20–25 cookies

Toffee almond crunch bars

This is a cookie from my childhood. The crunchy toffee-like base and milk chocolate topping are fabulous. Great for kids and the young of heart.

Ingredients

1 cup unblanched almonds
2 cups all-purpose flour
⅛ teaspoon salt
1 cup (2 sticks) unsalted butter

1 cup light brown sugar, tightly packed
1 egg
1 teaspoon vanilla extract
1½ cups chopped milk chocolate

Method

Preheat the oven to 350°F.

Place the almonds on a baking sheet and toast until golden. This will take about 15 minutes. Remove from the oven and allow to cool, then chop roughly. Set aside. Sift the flour and salt into a large bowl. In a separate bowl, cream the butter with the sugar until pale and fluffy. Add the egg and vanilla. Fold in the flour to make a sticky dough.

Using a metal spatula, spread the dough thinly over a 14 x 10½-inch baking sheet. Bake for 10–15 minutes, or until set and golden. Meanwhile, melt the chocolate in a double boiler or bowl set over a pan of hot water (or you can use a microwave). Remove the cookie base from the oven. Pour the melted chocolate over the top and sprinkle with the toasted nuts. Allow to cool completely before cutting into diamond or irregular shapes and serving.

Makes 30–40 bars

Snowballs

This is a very crumbly, buttery cookie rolled in confectioners' sugar, which just dissolves in your mouth (see picture overleaf). Snowballs were part of The Little Red Barn's very first product range. Sadly we had to take them off our list, because they didn't travel well – they used to arrive looking like a bag of flour. So for those of you who keep asking us when we'll be stocking these again, I'm afraid you'll just have to make them yourself. Here's the recipe.

Ingredients

2 cups all-purpose flour
⅛ teaspoon salt
¾ cup (1½ sticks) cold unsalted butter

½ cup ground almonds
1 teaspoon vanilla extract
Confectioners' sugar

Method

Sift the flour and salt into a large bowl. Cut the butter into small dice. Put the butter and sifted dry ingredients into a food processor. Whiz until the mixture resembles coarse meal. Pour the mixture back into the large bowl. Add the almonds and vanilla, and gather the mixture into a dough. Cover with plastic wrap and chill for about 1 hour.

Preheat the oven to 350°F.

Sift some confectioners' sugar into a medium bowl. Set aside. Pinch off pieces of dough the size of large marbles, roll into balls, and place on ungreased baking sheets. Continue until all the dough is used up. Bake for 10–12 minutes, or until set but not brown. Leave to cool on the baking sheets for a few minutes, then roll the warm cookies in the confectioners' sugar. Be gentle as they will be quite fragile. Transfer to a wire rack. Allow to cool completely before dusting with more confectioners' sugar and serving.

Makes 50–60 cookies

Chocolate truffle cookies

These cookies look stunning, and they don't require much preparation time. They're best made and eaten within the hour, which shouldn't be too much of a problem. I like to serve them as petits fours, at the end of a meal, with coffee. The good thing is you can make the dough ahead of time and bake the cookies at the very last minute for the full "wow! fresh cookies" effect.

Ingredients

½ cup all-purpose flour

½ cup granulated sugar

¼ cup unsweetened cocoa powder

½ teaspoon baking powder

¼ teaspoon salt

2 tablespoons unsalted butter

1 extra large egg

1 teaspoon Cognac

Confectioners' sugar

Method

Sift the flour, granulated sugar, cocoa, baking powder, and salt into a large bowl. Rub in the butter using your fingertips. Add the egg and Cognac, and mix well. Chill the dough in the freezer for about 20 minutes, until it's firm enough to handle.

Preheat the oven 400°F. Lightly grease two baking sheets.

Take a scoop of dough with a teaspoon and roll into a ball. Roll the ball in confectioners' sugar, then place on a prepared baking sheet, leaving room for spreading. Continue until all the dough is used up. Bake for 8–10 minutes, or until just set. Leave to cool on the baking sheets for a few minutes before transferring to a wire rack. Allow to cool completely before serving.

Makes 24 cookies

Empanaditas • Colombian aji • Cheese and anchovy puffs • Crisp-baked polenta sticks • Cheese crescents • Cream crackers • Oven-baked "fries" Garlicky mayonnaise • Spicy vegetable parcels • Pigs in blankets Toasted bread croutes • Miniature tartlet shells

Canapés, hors d'œuvres, and light snacks

Croustades • Crème fraîche and capers • Shrimp salad • Egg salad
Sesame choux puffs • Spicy gougères • Miniature pizza bases
Caramelized onion tartlets • Pepper jam tartlets • Dijon Parmesan hearts
Apricot and cherry chutney • Fresh tomato salsa

My mother has always been a terrific hostess. My earliest childhood memories were of her elaborate cocktail parties and elegant dinner parties. These special occasions always began with a sparkling assortment of canapés and hors d'œuvres.

She would start planning and organizing her menus weeks in advance. A long list of canapés would be taped to the refrigerator door, and my sisters and I would survey the list with a critical eye. Our favorites were anchovy puffs and pigs in blankets, both made with her very own homemade puff pastry. I used to watch with great admiration as she rolled out the pastry, always working from the center out, then folded it and turned it in some complicated manner before putting it in the fridge for a period of rest.

As the countdown to the big day approached, we kids either did our best to help, or we stayed well out of her way. My favorite job was to line up the canapés in neat little rows on the polished silver trays. Helping with the waitressing ran a close second. I took special pride in reciting to the guests in perfect English and Spanish what each item was.

My own style of entertaining is much more casual. I tend to forgo the obligatory first course and replace it with a selection of homemade nibbles. In today's pre-prepared world, where frozen canapés shout at you from every supermarket shelf, it's nice to show that you've made an effort and created something a little bit special for your guests.

Don't underestimate the pleasure that home-baking will bring. My repertoire includes many of my mother's creations along with a few inventions of my own. All of these can be made up quickly, on the spur of the moment, and many will double up as light appetizers or perhaps even a meal on their own.

Empanaditas

This is a classic snack served in Colombia. It's typically made with leftovers, either chicken or beef, and the pastry is made from whole corn that is soaked and ground by hand. I've sacrificed a bit of authenticity for the sake of speed here, but the results are still good. Serve the Empanaditas with some very authentic Colombian aji (see page 115), a seasoned chili vinegar, used throughout South America, or some Tabasco sauce.

You may want to consider making a batch of these and storing them in the freezer. They will be a lifesaver if you suddenly find yourself with impromptu guests at the weekend.

Ingredients

1 medium potato, peeled and finely diced

3 tablespoons olive oil

1 tablespoon unsalted butter

1 medium onion, minced

2 cloves of garlic, finely chopped

2 teaspoons dried oregano

1 teaspoon paprika

1 tablespoon ground cumin

2 medium tomatoes, skinned, seeded, and cut into small cubes

1 medium green sweet pepper, finely diced

8 ounces ground beef, pork, or chicken

¼ cup capers, coarsely chopped

Salt and freshly ground black pepper

1 tablespoon lime juice

1½ pounds frozen puff pastry, thawed

1 egg, lightly beaten

Method

Parboil the potato until just tender. Drain and set aside. While the potato is cooking, heat 2 tablespoons of the oil and the butter in a frying pan and fry the onion until translucent. Add the garlic, followed by the oregano, paprika, and cumin. Stir well. Fry for a few more minutes until fragrant. Add the tomatoes, green sweet pepper, and potatoes to the onion and spices, and heat through for a few minutes. Remove from the heat and pour the mixture into a large bowl. Leave to cool. In the same pan, fry the ground meat in the remaining oil. The idea is to cook the meat quickly and evaporate as much of the liquid as possible using a high heat. If at the end of cooking there is still some liquid in the pan, tip the meat into a colander to drain.

Add the meat to the onions, peppers, and tomatoes, along with the capers. The mixture should be moist but not liquidy. Add the lime juice, and season with salt and pepper to taste. Leave to cool. The filling can be made a day in advance and kept in the fridge.

(Continued on page 115)

Preheat the oven to 400°F.

Roll out the puff pastry to about ⅛ inch thick. Cut out rounds with a sharp 3½-inch cookie cutter. To shape an empanadita, put a heaping teaspoon of the filling mixture in the center of a pastry round. Holding the round in the center of your palm, gently fold it over in half. Be sure there are no air pockets, then pinch the edges together. Press the joined edge with the back of a fork to make a decorative seal and place on a baking sheet. Repeat this procedure until all the filling and pastry have been used. Brush the pastries with the lightly beaten egg. Bake for 12–15 minutes, or until golden. Serve hot.

Makes 40 empanaditas

★ **Note**: For vegetarian empanaditas, just leave out the meat.

Colombian aji

Ingredients

2 fresh hot red chili peppers, seeded
1 teaspoon salt
½ cup white wine vinegar
2 tablespoons minced onion

1 medium tomato, skinned, seeded, and cut into small chunks
2 tablespoons minced fresh cilantro
⅛ teaspoon granulated sugar

Method

Using a mortar and pestle, crush the chili peppers with the salt until they are almost a paste. Add the vinegar and stir. Leave the mixture to sit undisturbed for 30 minutes.

Add the onion, tomato, and cilantro to the vinegar and chili mixture. Add the sugar to balance out the flavor. Allow to stand for 15 minutes before serving.

Serves 6–8

Cheese and anchovy puffs

This is my mother's recipe. It made a regular appearance at nearly every cocktail party or bridge party I can remember. The good thing is that the puffs are really easy to make and they always get rave reviews, even from confirmed anchovy haters.

They can be assembled several days ahead of time and kept in the fridge or freezer prior to baking. If frozen, you don't need to thaw them before baking. Just put them straight into the oven.

Ingredients

2-ounce can anchovy fillets

8 ounces frozen puff pastry, thawed

½ cup finely diced cheese (Cheddar, Gruyère, or Edam)

1 egg yolk, mixed with 1 tablespoon cold water

¼ cup sesame seeds

Method

Remove the anchovies from their oil and gently blot with paper towels. Using scissors or a sharp knife, cut the anchovy fillets into 1-inch lengths. Set aside.

Roll out the puff pastry to a large rectangle about ⅛ inch thick. Cut out rounds using a 2½-inch cookie cutter. Top each round with a piece of cheese and one of anchovy. Fold the pastry over the filling and press the edges together to seal, curving into a crescent shape. Make sure there are no gaps for the cheese to escape. Use the back of a fork to press along the outer edge, making a decorative seal. Brush the top of each crescent with the egg yolk mixture and sprinkle with sesame seeds. Place the crescents on ungreased baking sheets. Chill in the fridge or freezer for at least 30 minutes before baking.

Preheat the oven to 400°F.

As your guests arrive, place the baking sheets in the hot oven and bake for 15 minutes, or until puffed and golden. Remove the puffs from the baking sheets and allow to cool on a serving dish for a few minutes before serving.

Makes 25–30 puffs

Crisp-baked polenta sticks

These are immensely satisfying to prepare and are always popular. They're baked in the oven so are relatively low in fat, making them a healthy alternative to deep-fried potato skins. Serve them with Fresh tomato salsa (see page 141), or with some chili sauce.

By the way, Oscar, our otherwise impeccably well-behaved chocolate Labrador, absolutely adores these. He has been known to succumb to stealing a stick or two when no one is watching. Who can blame him?

Ingredients

2 teaspoons salt

2½ cups quick-cooking polenta

1¼ cups freshly grated Parmesan cheese

½ cup (1 stick) unsalted butter

Salt and freshly ground black pepper

Olive oil

Method

To prepare the polenta, bring 2½ pints water to a boil, then add the salt. Now pour the polenta into the water in a steady stream, stirring constantly to prevent lumps from forming. Continue to stir the polenta over a gentle heat until it starts to come away from the sides of the pan. This will take about 5 minutes. The polenta is cooked when it's quite smooth (taste a bit). If it still feels gritty, cook for a few minutes longer, stirring to ensure that it doesn't burn or stick to the bottom of the pot.

When the polenta is cooked, remove from the heat and add the grated Parmesan and butter. Stir with a wooden spoon until well incorporated. Taste and season with salt and pepper accordingly. Pour the mixture onto a cool surface like a chopping board or a slab of marble. Shape into a rectangle and flatten out to about ½ inch thick. Leave to cool for 30 minutes. Once the polenta has cooled, you can wrap it up in plastic wrap and keep it in the fridge for a few days until you're ready to bake the sticks.

Preheat the oven to 350°F. Lightly grease two baking sheets with olive oil.

When the polenta is cool enough to handle, slice it into strips the size of thick fries. Place these, smooth-side down, on the baking sheets. Brush the tops with a little more olive oil. Bake for 20 minutes, or until the tops are golden and crunchy. Serve hot.

Makes 90–100 sticks

Cheese crescents

These homemade cheese crackers are light and flaky, and make good pre-dinner nibbles as they're not too filling. Have a little play with the amount of spice you use, and try caraway seeds, sesame seeds, or poppy seeds as alternative toppings. I like these with a hearty cayenne kick and sprinkled with fennel seeds.

Ingredients

1½ cups all-purpose flour
1 teaspoon salt
½ teaspoon cayenne
½ teaspoon baking powder
½ cup (1 stick) unsalted butter

2 eggs
1½ cups grated cheese (use any hard cheese like Parmesan or Cheddar)
1 egg white, mixed with 1 tablespoon water
2 tablespoons fennel seeds (optional)

Method

Combine the flour, salt, cayenne, and baking powder in a large mixing bowl. Rub the butter into the flour, using your fingertips, lifting the mixture above the bowl as you work to incorporate air and keep the mixture light. Make a well in the center and add the eggs and cheese. Gather the mixture into a dough and knead lightly. If the dough is too wet, add a little more flour so that it's easier to handle. Shape the dough into a disk and flatten it out slightly. Wrap the dough in plastic wrap and chill for a few hours.

Preheat the oven to 350°F.

Roll out the dough into a rectangle about ¼ inch thick. Fold the rectangle into thirds, then give the dough a quarter turn clockwise. Roll the dough out again, and repeat the folding and turning. Roll out the dough for a third time, into a rectangular shape about ⅛ inch thick. Cut out crescent shapes using a cookie cutter and place them on an ungreased baking sheet. Gently gather up the scraps, re-roll as necessary, and cut out more crescents. Don't re-roll the pastry more than twice or you'll lose some of the flaky texture.

Brush the crescents with a little of the egg white mixture and sprinkle with fennel seeds, if using. Bake for 15–20 minutes, or until crisp and golden. Transfer to wire racks and allow to cool for a few minutes before serving.

Makes 60 crescents

★ **Note:** Instead of a crescent-shaped cookie cutter, you could use a plain round 2-inch cookie cutter.

Cream crackers

These look nice, taste delicious and are very simple to make. Serve them as nibbles with drinks, with a range of dips, or at the end of a meal with cheese.

Ingredients

1 cup all-purpose flour
½ teaspoon salt
1 teaspoon granulated sugar

1 tablespoon unsalted butter
4 tablespoons light cream

Method

Preheat the oven to 300°F.

Sift the flour, salt, and sugar into a large bowl. Rub in the butter, using your fingertips, as if making pastry. Make a well in the center and add the cream. Mix lightly and gather up to make a soft dough. If the dough seems too dry, add a little more cream; if it's too wet, dust with a little extra flour. Handle the dough gently. Don't overwork.

Roll out the dough on a lightly floured surface to about ⅛ inch thick. Using a square cookie cutter or a knife, cut out 2-inch squares. Cut them close together as this dough shouldn't be rolled out more than once. Place the squares on an ungreased baking sheet and prick lightly with a fork all over to prevent the crackers from rising during baking. Bake for 15–20 minutes, or until just crisp. Allow to cool for a few minutes before serving.

Makes 20 crackers

Oven-baked "fries"

I came home from work one evening and discovered that the cupboard was bare, except for one lonely potato. Too hungry to wait for a baked potato, I sliced it up into wedges, skin and all, tossed it into a bowl with a few unpeeled cloves of garlic, drizzled them with a bit of olive oil, and seasoned with salt and pepper. Once baked, the results were very tasty and I've been dishing them up ever since. Serve these with drinks. Pile them in a large bowl, and offer a few dipping sauces too. They're delicious with Colombian aji (see page 115), or try them Belgian style, with a good beer and some Garlicky mayonnaise (see below).

Ingredients

4 medium potatoes
(suitable for roasting)

Salt and pepper

Olive oil

5–6 cloves of garlic, unpeeled (optional)

Method

Preheat the oven to 400°F.

Wash and scrub the potatoes. Dry thoroughly and cut into chunky ½-inch thick wedges. Put the wedges in a large bowl. Add salt and pepper to taste and a liberal drizzle of good-quality olive oil. If you're using garlic cloves, add them now. Give everything a good mix with your hands, ensuring that the potatoes are well coated with oil but not drenched.

Place the potatoes on a baking sheet, making sure they're all in one layer and not touching each other. Bake for 30–40 minutes, undisturbed, or until golden and crispy. Allow to cool for a few minutes before serving.

Serves 4

Garlicky mayonnaise

Ingredients

2 anchovy fillets

½ cup mayonnaise

1 clove of garlic, minced

1 teaspoon white wine vinegar

Salt and freshly ground black pepper

Method

Mash the anchovies with the back of a fork, to make a paste. Add this to the rest of the ingredients. Season with salt and pepper to taste.

Serves 4–6

Spicy vegetable parcels

Ingredients

1 small eggplant, cut into small cubes

4–6 tablespoons olive oil

2 medium potatoes, peeled and cut into small cubes

1 small onion, minced

2 cloves of garlic, minced

1 fresh hot chili pepper, seeded and minced

1½ teaspoon curry powder

½ teaspoon cayenne

1 teaspoon ground cumin

1 teaspoon ground coriander

1 teaspoon ground cinnamon

½ teaspoon salt

1 tomato, skinned, seeded, and diced

1 tablespoon lime juice

1–2 tablespoons hot lime pickle

14 ounces (12–14 sheets) frozen filo pastry, thawed

¼–½ cup unsalted butter, melted and cooled

Method

Preheat the oven to 400°F.

Place the eggplant in a roasting pan and drizzle with some of the olive oil. Roast in the oven for 15–20 minutes, or until tender. Meanwhile, cook the potatoes in boiling water until tender. Drain and set aside. Heat the remaining oil in a frying pan. Add the onion and fry until translucent. Add the garlic and chili pepper, and fry for a few more minutes. Add the ground spices and salt, and stir for a few minutes until fragrant. Remove from the heat. Add the eggplant and potatoes. Tip the mixture into a bowl and add the diced tomato, lime juice, and lime pickle. Blend lightly with a fork. Leave to cool. (The filling can be made up to 2 days ahead and kept in the fridge.)

To assemble the parcels, cut the pastry into long strips measuring about 4 x 11 inches. Brush one strip with melted butter, then place another strip across the first to form a cross. Brush the second strip with melted butter. Repeat the procedure, so that you now have two layers of pastry in each direction, each brushed with melted butter. Place a little mound of filling on the square where the strips intersect. Gather up the ends of the strips over the filling and pinch together to form a purse. Place the parcel on an ungreased baking sheet. Repeat with the remaining pastry and filling. At this point, you can refrigerate the pastries: wrap the baking sheets tightly in plastic wrap and put in the fridge. When your guests arrive, just unwrap and place straight in the hot oven.

Bake the parcels for 10–15 minutes, or until golden. Allow to cool for a few minutes before serving.

Makes 10–12 parcels

Pigs in blankets

I learned the hard way, during my catering years, that everyone loves sausage rolls more than any other canapé. Louise Cantrill, the designer of this book, and I discussed at great length what could be done to make the ordinary version a bit more special. Our collaborative efforts are incorporated below. I suggest you consider making double quantities, as these will disappear fast.

Ingredients

6 premium pork sausages
(or any other sausage of your choice)

1 recipe all-purpose pastry (see page 65)

Horseradish or cranberry sauce

1 egg, lightly beaten

Method

Using a sharp knife, cut the sausages into ½-inch chunks.

Roll out the pastry to a large rectangle about ⅛ inch thick. Cut out rectangular shapes, about 3 x 2½ inches. Place ½ teaspoon horseradish or cranberry sauce in the center of each rectangle and put a chunk of sausage on top. Fold the edges of the pastry together to enclose the filling completely. Press down to seal the edges. Cut two small vent holes in each parcel with the point of a sharp knife to form a snout. Brush the top of each parcel with a little beaten egg and place on an ungreased baking sheet. Refrigerate until needed.

Preheat the oven to 400°F.

Bake the pigs for 10–15 minutes, or until the pastry is golden. Reduce the oven temperature to 350°F and bake for a further 5 minutes to ensure the sausages are fully cooked. To test for doneness, insert a sharp knife into the middle of the parcel and hold it there for 5 seconds, then remove. If the point is too hot to hold against your skin, the pigs are cooked! Allow to cool for a few minutes before serving.

Makes 30–40 pigs in blankets

Toasted bread croutes

Select a good-quality sliced bread with a tasty flavor. The idea here is to dry out the croutes without browning them too much. You want a really crunchy, airy-textured croute that will transport the topping from plate to mouth, without incident.

Ingredients

16 slices of good bread (white, brown, brioche, sourdough, rye, or pumpernickel)

Method

Preheat the oven to 220°F.

Place the slices of bread on a chopping board. Cut out the desired shapes using a selection of canapé-sized pastry cutters, avoiding the crusts. Transfer the cut-outs to an ungreased baking sheet and place in the oven to dry out. This can take up to 45 minutes, depending on the type of bread used. Remove from the oven and transfer to a wire rack to cool. Store in an airtight container.

Makes about 64 croutes

Miniature tartlet shells

Miniature tartlet shells are an ideal container for a variety of fillings. Select from a range of sweet or savory mixtures and let your creative juices run wild.

Ingredients

1 recipe all-purpose pastry (see page 65)

Method

On a lightly floured surface, roll out the dough to an even rectangle. The thickness depends on you. I prefer a thinnish layer of pastry, about ⅛ inch thick or less. Cut rounds from the rolled pastry to suit the size of the 1½-inch tartlet molds. Gently coax the dough into the molds, being careful to avoid tearing. Line the pastry shells with miniature paper cups filled with ceramic baking beans or dried pulses. Chill for 15–20 minutes, or until ready to bake.

Preheat the oven to 375°F.

Bake the pastry shells for 6–8 minutes. Remove the paper cups and beans, and put the pastry shells back into the oven to bake for a few more minutes until the pastry is set. Leave to cool in the molds for a few minutes, then transfer to a wire rack to cool completely. Handle the pastry shells carefully as they are fragile.

Makes 60 miniature tartlet shells

Croustades

This is a very easy recipe I picked up during my time at Leith's School of Food and Wine. The croustades are delicious just on their own, served with a range of dips. They also make great bases for lots of toppings, and you can even float them on soup. Be sure to use a good-quality olive oil to get the best flavor.

Ingredients

About ½ cup olive oil
1 large French baguette

Method

Preheat the oven to 300°F. Lightly grease a baking sheet with olive oil.

Pour some olive oil onto a small plate. Cut the bread into slices about ⅛ inch thick. Take each slice of baguette and quickly dip one side in the oil, being careful not to saturate it. Place the bread, oil-side up, on the baking sheet.

Bake the croustades for 15–20 minutes, or until lightly golden, dry, and crunchy. Watch them carefully as they can burn easily. Transfer to a wire rack to cool.

Store in an airtight container or freeze them until ready to use.

Makes about 30 croustades

 ## Topping ideas:

- Caramelized onions (see page 137) and goat's cheese, garnished with fresh thyme
- Pepper jam (see page 138) with anchovies and capers
- Goat's cheese and Apricot and cherry chutney (see page 141)
- Tomato and arugula, drizzled with olive oil
- Smoked salmon with Crème fraîche and capers (see page 129)
- Egg salad (see page 131) with fresh herbs

Crème fraîche and capers

Don't let the simplicity of this filling and an aversion to capers prevent you from trying this. It's bliss! It makes a very pretty canapé, with the white and green contrasting nicely with other more colorful canapé offerings. White or brown toasted bread croutes (see page 126) make ideal bases.

Ingredients

30 capers

3 tablespoons crème fraîche (or sour cream)

3 tablespoons whipping cream

½ cup whipped cream cheese

Salt and freshly ground black pepper

Paprika, for sprinkling

Method

Using a pair of scissors, snip each caper almost in half lengthwise, and gently pull the two ends out so that they resemble the petals of a flower. Set aside.

Combine the crème fraîche, whipping cream, and cream cheese in a bowl. Taste and season with salt and pepper as required.

To assemble the canapés, pile a teaspoon of the crème fraîche mixture on top of each croute. Top with a caper and sprinkle with a little paprika. Serve immediately.

Makes enough for 30 croutes

Shrimp salad

This makes a luxurious canapé topping. Serve in Miniature tartlet shells (see page 126) or on Toasted bread croutes (see page 126). Have the filling ready and well chilled, and assemble the canapés just before serving.

Ingredients

8 ounces freshly cooked jumbo shrimp, peeled and deveined

2 tablespoons mayonnaise

1 teaspoon whole-grain mustard

5–8 French cornichons, diced

Salt and freshly ground black pepper

Squeeze of lemon juice

Dash of Tabasco sauce

Fresh herbs (such as dill, chervil or flat-leaf parsley), to garnish

Method

Make sure the shrimp are thoroughly dried. Add the mayonnaise, mustard, cornichons, and salt and pepper to taste. Sharpen with a little lemon juice and Tabasco. Chill until ready to use.

Makes enough for 4–6 as an appetizer or 20 canapés

Egg salad

It's difficult to explain how nice it is to eat something as simple as a well-made egg salad. Use the freshest eggs and, if possible, herbs grown in your garden.

Ingredients

4 eggs

4 tablespoons mayonnaise

1 teaspoon Dijon mustard

¼ cup finely diced celery

Pinch of cayenne (optional)

Salt and freshly ground black pepper

Fresh herbs (such as chervil, chives, or flat-leaf parsley), to garnish

Method

Fill a saucepan with cold water and add the eggs. Bring to a boil, then set your timer for 10 minutes. After 10 minutes, drain off the hot water and immediately refresh the eggs with cold water. Leave to cool for a few minutes before peeling.

Using the back of a fork, mash the eggs until quite fine. Add the mayonnaise, mustard, celery, cayenne, and salt and pepper to taste. Place on your chosen base, being careful not to overload the filling. Garnish with fresh herbs.

Makes enough for 4 sandwiches or 30 canapés

Sesame choux puffs

Choux makes delicious containers for lots of interesting fillings. Here's the basic pastry recipe which you can experiment with to make as plain or as exciting as you wish. Try adding either ½–1 teaspoon chili powder, ½ teaspoon fennel or caraway seeds, or 1 tablespoon finely chopped herbs, such as chives, dill, or parsley, to the dough together with the sesame seeds.

Ingredients

6 tablespoons unsalted butter
¾ cup + 1 tablespoon all-purpose flour
3 eggs, lightly beaten

¼ cup sesame seeds
½ teaspoon salt

Method

Put 1 cup water and the butter in a saucepan, and bring to a rapid boil over a high heat. By the time the water has boiled, the butter should have melted. As soon as the mixture starts to boil, remove from the heat and quickly stir in the flour. Beat the mixture with a wooden spoon until it forms a smooth paste. Spoon the paste out of the saucepan onto a flat plate. Allow to cool for 10–15 minutes. Once cool, tip the paste into a mixing bowl. Add the eggs by thirds, stirring vigorously until you have a shiny, smooth, and velvety mixture. Add the sesame seeds and salt.

Preheat the oven to 425°F.

Drop teaspoonfuls of the dough onto an ungreased baking sheet. Bake for 10–15 minutes, depending on size, or until well risen and golden. Insert a wooden cocktail stick into each puff to allow some of the hot steam to escape. Reduce the oven temperature to 350°F and place them back in the oven for 5 minutes to dry out slightly.

To fill, slice off the top of each puff. Fill and replace the lid at a jaunty angle. Alternatively, make a small hole on the side of the puff. Spoon your filling into a pastry bag, insert the nozzle into the hole, and pipe in the filling.

Makes 50 bite-size puffs

 ## Filling ideas:

- Caviar and sour cream
- Pâté and Apricot and cherry chutney (see page 141)
- Thai-style chicken salad, garnished with fresh cilantro
- Egg salad (see page 131) with fresh chives
- Shrimp salad (see page 131)
- Marc's rum-flavored whipped cream (see page 75), drizzled with caramel

Spicy gougères

Gougère is a savory version of a cream puff. These are buttery, with a distinct Gruyère flavor and a hint of spiciness. They smell heavenly. Guests have been known to migrate to the kitchen on the pretence of helping, just to see what's in the oven. Serve these snacks on a winter evening while sitting in front of a roaring fire. For drinks, I recommend a classic buttery chardonnay, a good beaujolais, or some rioja.

Ingredients

6 tablespoons unsalted butter
¾ cup + 1 tablespoon all-purpose flour
3 eggs, lightly beaten
¼ cup sesame seeds
1 teaspoon Dijon mustard

1 teaspoon chili powder
½–1 teaspoons salt, as required
½ teaspoon freshly ground black pepper
½ cup Gruyère cheese, cut into small cubes

Method

Put 1 cup water and the butter in a saucepan, and bring to a rapid boil over a high heat. By the time the water has boiled, the butter should have melted. As soon as the mixture starts to boil, remove from the heat and quickly stir in the flour. Beat the mixture with a wooden spoon until it forms a smooth paste. Spoon the paste out of the saucepan onto a flat plate. Allow to cool for 10–15 minutes. Once cool, tip the paste into a mixing bowl. Add the eggs by thirds, stirring vigorously until you have a shiny, smooth, and velvety mixture. Add the sesame seeds, mustard, chili powder, salt, pepper and Gruyère. Taste for seasoning and adjust as necessary.

Preheat the oven to 425°F.

Drop tablespoonfuls of the dough onto an ungreased baking sheet. Bake for 10–15 minutes, or until well risen and golden. Insert a wooden cocktail stick into each gougère to allow some of the hot steam to escape. Reduce the oven temperature to 350°F and place them back in the oven for 5 minutes to dry out slightly.

Serve straight away, or leave them to cool and then freeze for later use. If frozen, there's no need to thaw them before reheating just put them straight into a 400°F oven to warm through.

Makes 30 gougères

Miniature pizza bases

These make a substantial hors d'œuvre, and they're nice for a light lunch or casual supper, served with a green salad. Keep your toppings simple, but use top notch ingredients.

Ingredients

Pinch of granulated sugar   1 teaspoon salt
1½ teaspoons active dry yeast   ¼ cup olive oil
2 cups unbleached flour

Method

Put ¾ cup water in a saucepan and heat until lukewarm. Combine the sugar and yeast in a small bowl and add ¼ cup of the lukewarm water. Stir gently to dissolve. Allow to sit for 5–10 minutes. The mixture should be creamy with a foamy top. If after 10 minutes there is no creamy foam on the yeast mixture, it means one of two things: the yeast you're using is old and needs replacing, or the water was too hot and has killed the yeast. Throw the yeast mixture away and start again with fresh yeast.

Sift the flour and salt into a large bowl. Make a well in the center. Add the yeast mixture, the rest of the water, and the olive oil. Mix together to form a nice, soft and pliable dough. If the dough is very sticky, add more flour. Knead for about 5 minutes until soft and silky.

Lightly grease a large bowl with some olive oil. Place the dough in the bowl and turn to coat with oil. Cover with plastic wrap and leave to rise until doubled in size. This can take anywhere from 45 minutes to 1½ hours.

When the dough is well risen, punch it down, and leave to rest for a few minutes. Meanwhile, lightly grease a baking sheet and sprinkle with a little corn meal or polenta. Roll out the dough to about ⅛ inch thick. Cut out rounds with a 2-inch cookie cutter. Flatten these out with a rolling pin and place on the prepared baking sheet. Gather up the scraps of dough and knead together gently for a few minutes. Leave the dough to rest for a few minutes before rolling out and cutting more rounds. Preheat the oven to 425°F. Add your chosen toppings to the pizza bases and drizzle with a little olive oil. Bake for 5–10 minutes, or until crisp and golden. Serve immediately.

Makes 15–20 miniature pizza bases

 ## Topping ideas:

- Anchovies, fresh oregano, and slivers of Parmesan

- Roasted red sweet peppers, olives, and capers

- Roast potatoes, Parmesan, and arugula

- Prosciutto, Parmesan, and arugula

Caramelized onion tartlets

The onion jam used in these tartlets is both sweet and savory. It requires a bit of preparation time, but the results are well worth it.

For the tartlets

1¼ cups whipping cream
4 extra large egg yolks
Salt and freshly ground black pepper
8 individual pre-baked tartlet shells, made with all-purpose pastry (see pages 65 and 126)

For the onion jam

½ cup (1 stick) unsalted butter
4 large onions, thinly sliced
1 teaspoon salt

Method

To make the onion jam, melt the butter in a large frying pan, preferably one with a tight-fitting lid. Add the onions and gently stir to mix. Trace out a circle 12 inches in diameter on a sheet of parchment paper and cut it out. Crumple the paper circle and hold it under the cold tap to soak through. Gently open the paper and lay it across the onions in the frying pan. Tuck the ends of the paper in slightly, then cover the pan with a tight-fitting lid. If you don't have a lid, cover the pan with a baking sheet and put a heavy pot on top. You want to create steam inside the pan so the onions sweat very slowly. Leave on a gentle heat for about 45 minutes – the longer the better. Check every once in a while to make sure the onions are not sticking to the bottom of the pan. If you're having a peek, remember to put the parchment paper and the lid back on tightly.

At the end of 45 minutes you should have some very soft onions with a fair amount of liquid. Remove the paper and lid, and increase the heat slightly. Add the salt and continue to cook uncovered, stirring every once in a while, until the onions are a deep caramel color. The end result should look like a thick jam of caramelized onion. Remove from the heat and leave to cool, then place the onion jam in a bowl. Store in the fridge until you're ready to use it.

Preheat the oven to 350°F.

To make the tartlets, mix together the cream, egg yolks, and salt and pepper to taste in a large bowl. Add the onion jam and mix lightly with a fork. Spoon the mixture into the tartlet shells, filling them generously. Place the tartlets on an ungreased baking sheet and bake for 15–20 minutes, or until the filling is set and golden.

Makes 8 individual tartlets

★ Note: For canapé-size tartlets, use 48 pre-baked Miniature tartlet shells made with all-purpose pastry (see pages 65 and 126). Place a teaspoonful of onion jam in the bottom of each and top with a little of the cream and egg yolk mixture. Bake for 6–8 minutes, or until the filling is set and golden.

Pepper jam tartlets

This little gem hails from my sister Dalia who lives in New York. During one particularly busy catering period, she agreed to come and help me. We slaved away for days and days in my kitchen in Silchester, and she was only allowed out to help with the deliveries. Not surprisingly, she's never wanted to come back to Silchester again.

This jam keeps well and you can use it for lots of different things. It makes an excellent omelette filling, is delicious with baked potatoes, and is particularly handy for canapés. Make the filling several days or even weeks in advance.

For the pepper jam

½ cup (1 stick) unsalted butter
4 tablespoons olive oil
6 red sweet peppers, thinly sliced
1 large onion, thinly sliced
2 teaspoons dried herbes de Provence
(or mixed thyme, rosemary and oregano)
Fresh basil, finely shredded

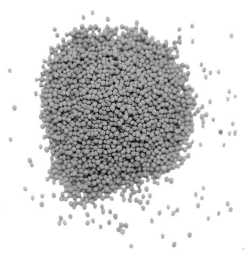

For the tartlets

12 individual or 48 canapé-sized pre-baked tartlet cases, made with all-purpose pastry (see pages 65 and 126)
12 or 48 anchovy fillets
12 or 48 capers
Fresh basil or thyme, to garnish

Method

To make the pepper jam, heat the butter and oil in a heavy saucepan. Add the peppers, onions and dried herbs, and stir through. Cook over a gentle heat for about 45 minutes–1 hour, stirring every once in a while.

At the end of the cooking time the mixture should be quite soft and there may be a lot of oil. If this is the case, spoon some of the oil out and turn up the heat. Continue to cook the mixture until most of the oil has disappeared. The mixture is ready when has the consistency of a thick jam. Remove from the heat and fold in the fresh basil. Leave to cool, then pack into a clean jar or bowl. Set aside until ready to use.

To assemble the tartlets, place a teaspoonful of jam in each pastry shell. Top with a slice of anchovy and a caper, and garnish with some fresh basil or thyme.

Makes 12 individual or 48 canapé-size tartlets

Dijon Parmesan hearts

These hearts are a good alternative to purchased cheese straws or other crackers. They look impressive and are a cinch to make. I like to serve them with icy-cold glasses of beer or a good chablis.

Ingredients

8 ounces frozen puff pastry, thawed
6 tablespoons coarse-grain Dijon mustard
½ cup freshly grated Parmesan cheese

Method

Preheat the oven to 400°F.

Roll out the pastry to a large rectangle about 12 x 15 inches and ⅛ inch thick. Spread the mustard evenly over the pastry and sprinkle with the grated Parmesan. Mark the middle of the longest side of the rectangle then, starting at one short end of the rectangle, roll up the pastry tightly. When you reach the middle, stop, and roll up the other half of the rectangle in the same way. You should now have two pastry cylinders touching each other, looking a bit like the Dead Sea scrolls. Using a sharp knife, cut the paired rolls across into 12–15 slices about ⅛ inch thick. Lay the slices flat on an ungreased baking sheet, cut-side up. Bake for 10–12 minutes, or until the pastry is crisp and dry. Serve hot or cold.

Makes 12–15 hearts

Apricot and cherry chutney

This is a quick chutney that goes well with just about anything. The end result should be glossy and fruity, with a little tang. For a quick snack, put some of this chutney on goat's cheese and toast. Mmmm!

Ingredients

¾ cup cider vinegar
4 tablespoons honey
1¼ teaspoons mustard seeds
Pinch of salt

2 x 1-inch chunks fresh gingerroot, peeled and smashed
1 fresh jalapeño chili (red or green), minced
½ cup dried sour cherries
1½ cups dried apricots, cut into chunks

Method

Combine the vinegar, honey, mustard seeds, salt, ginger, and chilli in a small saucepan. Cook on a high heat until the liquid is reduced to about one-third of its original volume. Add the dried cherries and cook for 3–4 minutes until the liquid is further reduced. Add the apricots and stir through. Continue cooking for a few minutes until almost all of the liquid has been absorbed or evaporated. The fruit should still be firm, not mushy. Remove from the heat. Pick out the large chunks of ginger and discard them. Place the chutney in a bowl and leave to cool. It will keep for up to 1 week in the fridge.

Serves 6–8

Fresh tomato salsa

Dips and sauces are always nicer made at home. Next time you need a zippy condiment, try making this salsa. It takes very little time to prepare, and is far superior to anything you can buy in a jar.

Ingredients

6 medium plum tomatoes, seeded and diced
½ medium onion, finely diced
1 fresh hot chili pepper, seeded and minced
Juice of 2 limes

½ teaspoon salt
Pinch of granulated sugar
⅓ cup minced fresh cilantro

Method

Mix together the diced tomato, onion, and chili. Add the lime juice, salt, and sugar. Add the cilantro and mix through. Leave to stand for at least 15 minutes before serving.

Serves 4–6

Index

Numbers in **bold** refer to photographs

all-purpose pastry.....................65
almond
  Raspberry and almond
    brownies 90
  Snowballs 107, **108**
  Toffee almond crunch bars 106
anchovy
  Cheese and anchovy puffs 116
  Garlicky mayonnaise 122
apple
  Apple, cranberry, and
    pecan loaf 56, **57**
  Apple pie 68
  Apple strudel 77
  Holiday pie 76
Apple, cranberry, and
  pecan loaf 56, **57**
Apple pie 68
Apple strudel 77
apricot
  Apricot and cherry chutney ..**140**, 141
  Apricot, pistachio, and
    cranberry bread 51
Apricot and cherry chutney **140**, 141
Apricot, pistachio, and
  cranberry bread 51
Aunt Ruthie's cheesecake 43

baking pans 11
banana
  Banana cream pie....................72
  Banana rock cakes 42
  Banana strudel **78**, 79
  Beth's banana maple
    muffins 16, **17**
  Classic banana bread 52, **53**
  Holiday pie 76
Banana cream pie.....................72
Banana rock cakes 42
Banana strudel **78**, 79
Barbara's pecan dainties 96
basic techniques 9
Bennington Diner,
  Bennington, Vermont...........14, 19
Beth's banana maple muffins 16, **17**
Blueberry muffins with
  struesel topping 15
brownies 86–91
Burnt butter frosting.........38, 39, 47
butter 10
Buttercream frosting 36, 45, 46
Buttermilk cherry muffins 18

cakes 30–45
canapés, hors d'œuvres, and
  light snacks 112–141
capers
  Crème fraîche and capers **128**, 129
Caramelized onion
  tartlets.....................**136**, 137
Carrot graffiti cake 40, **41**

Cheddar cheese scones 23
cheese
  Cheddar cheese scones 23
  Cheese and anchovy puffs 116
  Cheese crescents 118, **119**
  Crisp-baked polenta sticks.........117
  Dijon Parmesan hearts 139
Cheese and anchovy puffs 116
cheesecake
  Aunt Ruthie's cheesecake 43
  Cheesecake swirl brownies 91
Cheesecake swirl brownies 91
Cheese crescents 118, **119**
cherry
  Buttermilk cherry muffins 18
  Jumbo cherry scones 22
chili
  Colombian aji 115
  Fresh tomato salsa 141
chocolate 10, 33
  Banana rock cakes 42
  Cheesecake swirl brownies 91
  Chocolate buttercream
    frosting 46
  Chocolate chip cake 34
  Chocolate cream frosting...........47
  Chocolate truffle cookies **108**, 109
  Devil's food cake **32**, 33
  Double chocolate brownies.........87
  Marble loaf cake 35
  Peanut butter brownies.........**88**, 89
  Raspberry and almond
    brownies 90
  Rum and raisin brownies...........87
  Shrimpy's chocolate cake 31
chocolate brownies 8, 86, 87
Chocolate buttercream
  frosting 33, 46
Chocolate cream frosting......31, 34, 47
Chocolate truffle cookies **108**, 109
Cinnamon buns 24, **25**
Classic banana bread 52, **53**
Coconut cream pie 69
coffee..............................82–3
  Marc's 45-minute espresso 83
  Perfect coffee 82
  Polly's Mom's peanut cookies.........100
Colombian aji 115, 122
cookies 94–109
Corn bread 60
Corn muffins 19
cranberry
  Apple, cranberry, and
    pecan loaf 56, **57**
  Apricot, pistachio, and
    cranberry bread 51
Cream cheese frosting 41, 47
Cream crackers................**120**, 121
creaming 9
Crème fraîche and capers **128**, 129
Crisp-baked polenta sticks...........117
Croustades.........................127
Crumb crust 73

dairy products 10
Dalia's luscious lemon bars 95
Date bread 55
Devil's food cake **32**, 33
Dijon Parmesan hearts 139
Double chocolate brownies 86, 87

Easy-Bake Oven.....................6, 8
Easy vanilla-bean custard..............80
eggplant
  Spicy vegetable parcels 123
Egg salad 130
eggs 10
Empanaditas 113–15, **114**
equipment 11
folding 9
Fresh tomato salsa 141
frostings 46–7

garlic
  Garlicky mayonnaise 122
Garlicky mayonnaise 122
ginger
  Ginger crisps 100
  Pumpkin gingerbread...............59
Ginger crisps 100

Hesh's bakery, Philadelphia............34
Holiday pie 76
honey
  Traditional honey cake 39

Jumbo cherry scones 22

Key lime pie 73
kneading 9

leavening agents 10
Leith's School of
  Food and Wine 7, 127
lemon
  Dalia's luscious lemon bars 95
  Lemon buttercream frosting 46
  Lemon drizzle frosting 54
  Lemon meringue pie **70**, 71
  Lemon tea bread 54
Lemon buttercream frosting 46
Lemon drizzle frosting 54
Lemon meringue pie **70**, 71
Lemon tea bread 54
lime
  Key lime pie 73

maple
  Beth's banana maple muffins 16, **17**
  Maple butter cookies 97
  Maple buttercream frosting 46
  Vermont maple cake 38
Maple butter cookies 97
Maple buttercream frosting 46
Marble loaf cake 35
Marc's 45 minute espresso 54, 83
Marc's rum-flavored

whipped cream 75, 76
Miniature pizza bases 134, **135**
Miniature tartlet shells 127
Mrs J's molasses cookies 101
muffins 14–19

New Year's Day fruit cake 44, **45**

onion
   Caramelized onion tarts **136**, 137
   Onion jam.......................... 137
Onion jam........................... 137
organization.......................... 11
Oven-baked "fries" 122

pastry 10, 65
   all-purpose pastry................... 65
   puff 112
peanut
   Peanut butter brownies.......... 88, **89**
   Polly's Mom's peanut cookies 100
   Peanut butter brownies.......... 88, **89**
pecan
   Barbara's pecan dainties 96
   Pecan pie **74**, 75
   Apple, cranberry, and
   pecan loaf 56, **57**
   Pecan pie **74**, 75
Pepper jam 138
Pepper jam tartlets 138
Perfect coffee 82
Perfect whipped cream 80, **81**
pies and strudels 64–76
Pigs in blankets **124**, 125
pistachio
   Apricot, pistachio, and
   cranberry bread 51

Polly's Mom's peanut cookies 100
Popovers **26**, 27
pork
   Pigs in blankets **124**, 125
potato
   Empanaditas 113–15, **114**
   Oven-baked "fries".................. 122
   Spicy vegetable parcels 123
pumpkin
   Pumpkin gingerbread 59
   Pumpkin pie **66**, 67
   Savory pumpkin bread 61
Pumpkin gingerbread 59
Pumpkin pie **66**, 67

quick breads 50–61
Raspberry and almond
   brownies 90
Rindelaub's bakery,
   Philadelphia 24
Rolled sugar cookies 102, **103**
rubbing 9
rum
   Holiday pie 76
   Marc's rum-flavored
   whipped cream 75
   New Year's Day fruit cake 44, **45**
   Rum and raisin brownies............ 87
Rum and raisin brownies............. 87

salt 10
Savory pumpkin bread 61
scones........................... 21–23
Sesame choux puffs 132
shrimp
   Shrimp salad 130, **131**
Shrimp salad 130, **131**

Shrimpy's chocolate cake 31
Snickerdoodles 98, **99**
Snowballs 107, **108**
Soft and crumbly
   oatmeal cookies **104**, 105
Spicy gougères..................... 133
Spicy vegetable parcels 123
Swampscott baking
   powder biscuits................. **20**, 21
staple ingredients 10
strudels 77–79

The Little Red Barn ..8, 68, 86, 107, 142
Toasted bread croutes 126
Toffee and almond
   crunch bars 106
tomato
   Empanaditas 113–15, **114**
   Colombian aji 115
   Fresh tomato salsa 141
   Spicy vegetable parcel 123
topping ideas for canapés 127
Traditional honey cake 39

vanilla................................ 10
   Buttercream frosting 46
   Marble loaf cake 35
   Velvet butter cupcakes 36, **37**
Velvet butter cupcakes 36, **37**
Vermont maple cake 38

whisking 9

zucchini
   Zucchini and poppy seed loaf 58
Zucchini and poppy seed loaf 58

The Little Red Barn

For those of you who have not had the opportunity to try The Little Red Barn's mail order service, I hope this book will encourage you to give us a call. Our specialities include the squidgiest chocolate brownies, crisp buttery chocolate chip cookies, and our very own original 'swirl' biscotti, available in a range of flavors. Perfect to give as gifts or to send to yourself. So if you're pressed for time, you've forgotten someone's birthday, or it's just too hot to bake, give us a call. You can find us at:

Unit 5, Fronds Park, Frouds Lane, Aldermaston, Berkshire RG7 4LH
Tel: +44 (0)118 971 4322; Fax: +44 (0)118 971 4515
www.littleredbarn.co.uk; redbarn@dial.pipex.com

We look forward to hearing from you.